Lee Hansen
432-4762

To See

From

Sun

W9-DFF-655

PICTORIAL GUIDE TO
Hardy Perennials

John K. Drew

ISBN 0-89484-091-6   Hardcover
Library of Congress Card No. 84-61212

Published 1984 by
Merchants Publishing Co., Kalamazoo, MI.

Merchants Publishing Company
20 Mills Street, Kalamazoo, Michigan 49001

Printed in United States of America

FOREWORD

Pictorial Guide to Hardy Perennials is an attempt to show and describe common perennials that are available in retail greenhouses and garden centers throughout North America. Most are reliable performers under a wide range of soil and climatic conditions, providing common sense gardening practices are employed. More than 250 perennials are illustrated in full color photographs. Where possible, outstanding varieties and cultivars have been described.

We have made no attempt to present a history of these plants, provide a treatise on various propagation techniques or other subjects of interest only to the serious hobbyist.

Rather, our goal has been to show the diversity of perennial plant life, provide basic planting guidelines and help you decide where best to employ these plants in your landscape scheme.

TABLE OF CONTENTS...

ACKNOWLEDGEMENTS...

The author wishes to thank Dennis, John, David and Mary Walters, Walter's Gardens, Zeeland, Michigan for their help in the preparation of this book. PHOTO CREDITS: Derek Fell: 32, 33, 35, 48, 53, 54, 60, 65, 72, 79, 82, 86, 87, 89; Gottlieb Hampfler: front cover, 5, 6, 8, 10, 11, 12, 13, 17, 23, 46, 60; Muriel & Arthur Orans: 29, 53, 69, 73, 78; Stephen Still: 22, 27, 34, 49, 66; and Michael Warren: 18, 19, 21, 25, 26, 29, 30, 32, 34, 35, 36, 39, 41, 42, 43, 47, 49, 51, 53, 56, 58, 61, 62, 66, 67, 70, 71, 72, 73, 75, 76, 77, 79, 83, 84, 87, 88, and 92.

INTRODUCTION TO PERENNIALS

Diversity of growth habit, cultural needs, blooming periods and flower styles make perennials the most accommodating class of plants for the home landscape. How _you_ make use of them will depend on need, the proposed planting site and your creativity.

In contrast to annuals, which complete their life cycle in a year, and biennials, that are planted one year and flower the next, herbaceous perennials reappear each spring.

Depending on species and planting conditions, life span may only be for several seasons, yet a number of perennials may provide garden color for a decade or longer. Notable for their durability are Chinese Peonies, a clump of which may flourish for 30 years. At the other end of the spectrum are Delphiniums, which are spectacular for several seasons, but eventually lose their vigor and must be replaced. However, the beauty of their blooms and screening qualities make Delphiniums popular border plants.

GROWTH HABIT DIFFERS

In addition to varying life spans, perennials differ in other ways. Foremost is a wide diversity in growth habit. Probably no class of plant is represented by such a range in height, flower and foliage styles.

There are tall stately perennials that grow 8 feet or more, yet others creep over the ground, growing just 3-4 inches tall. Between these extremes is a myriad of perennials in varying shapes and sizes.

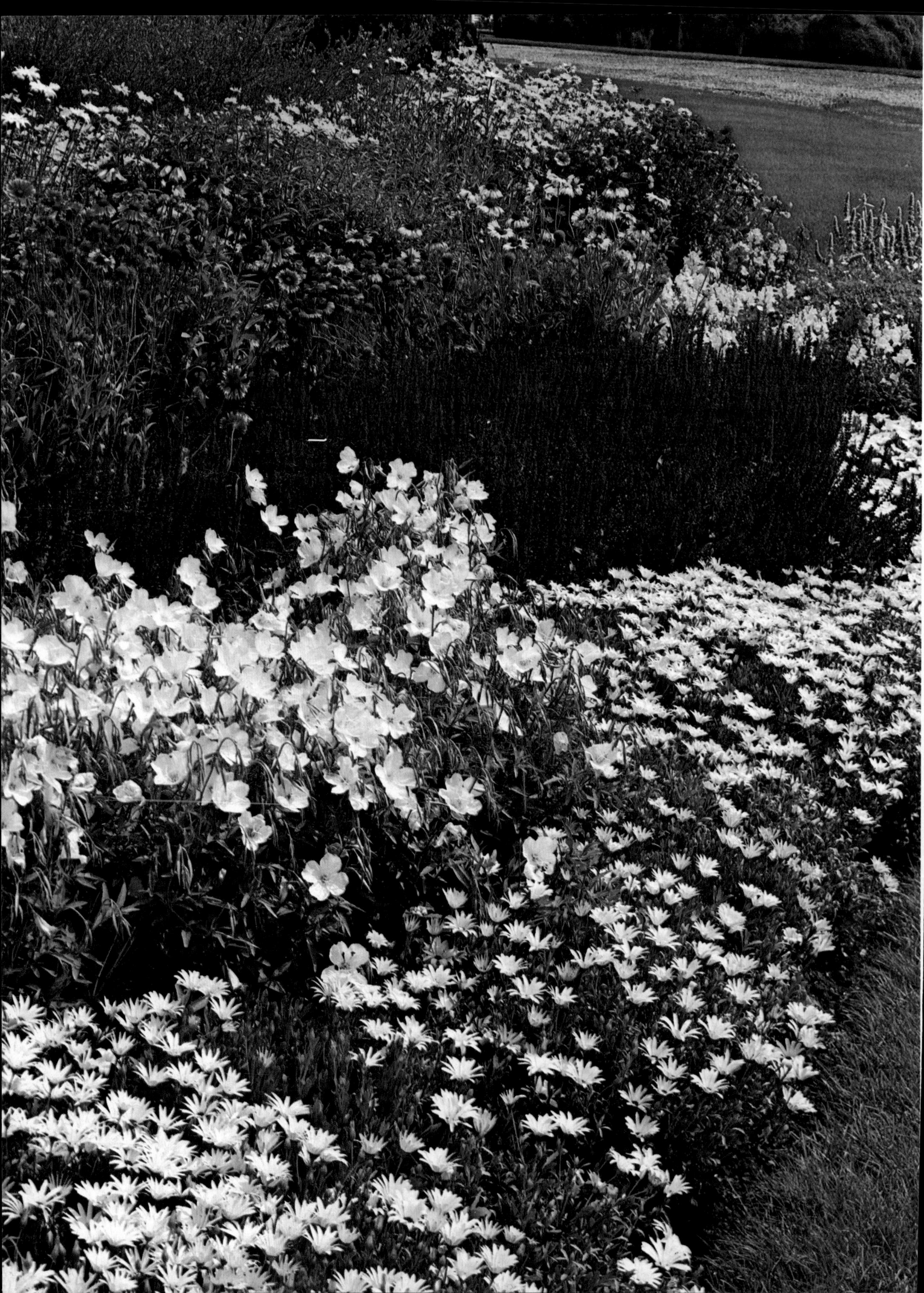

MO
(Sp)
(F) =
Ae
Ac
A
A

Foliage styles range from the simple grasslike leaves of Dianthus to the more complex, lobed, but deeply cut leaves of Shasta Daisy. Nearly every shade of green is represented and a number of perennials display their foliage throughout winter months. Foliage of many perennials is variegated, with gold or ivory providing a two-toned effect. Sometimes leaves are striped, while other have golden or ivory margins. Such foliage gives plants an ornamental quality before and after flowering.

Flowers are produced in nearly all colors of the rainbow. Some grow as tall spikes; others in daisy form. Star, cup, bell, globe, tube, powderpuff, spider and variations of these bloom shapes also can create interest in the garden from early spring until frost.

Accompanying differences in appearance are degrees as to how each species can adapt to various planting sites. Ancestors of modern perennials originated in nearly all vegetated areas of the earth. As a result, each has specific cultural needs. For instance, a perennial originating on a gravelly mountain ledge will not do well in a shaded bog soil. However, a sandy garden soil exposed to full sun will likely be a suitable planting site.

This same principle applies as to how well a plant may endure winter. Plants having developed in areas where soil rarely freezes will probably not survive where temperatures drop to 0° F. or below. Fortunately, a wide range of perennials can be grown where winters are cold. These are the ones primarily found in garden centers and mail order catalogs because of their adaptability. Most of these are featured in this book.

Because of the many differences in appearance and cultural requirements, perennials can be used to meet a wide range of planting needs. Some varieties may lend themselves to a flower border, while others may look best in the rock garden. A number of perennials make good groundcovers and still others find best use as foreground to a bed or border. Perennial uses are explored more deeply on pages 9-16. Recommendations for combining perennials with other plants in the garden are found on pages 90-95.

Whatever the planting situation, perennials give a sense of permanence to the garden. Similar to trees, shrubs and conifers in the landscape, perennials give a garden shape. Therefore, the basic framework of the flower border or rock garden should rest with perennials. Annuals and bulbs can be planted in special pockets, however, and replaced periodically during the growing season once blooms fade.

BASIC PLANT NEEDS

Most perennials like well-drained soil relatively high in organic content and available plant foods. Mulching with rotted bark, peat moss or other organic material will improve the air/water relationship in the soil. Surface applications of an all-around garden fertilizer three times during the year will provide adequate amounts of plant food. One application should be made in late autumn to help plants overwinter. Another should be made in early spring while plants are dormant and the third six weeks into the growing season. One more application can be made in late summer, although not mandatory, unless a plant is an autumn flowering variety.

Most perennials also perform better the following spring if an application of straw, leaves or evergreen boughs has been made in late autumn to protect against winter damage. The need for protection is greatest where the planting site is at the northern limit of a variety's hardiness rating. Such ratings have been included for each perennial listed on pages 18-88 and a USDA Hardiness Zone Map shown on page 98 can help gardeners determine what perennials will survive in their locales.

Although perennials are more expensive in the garden center than annual bedding plants, they are generally larger. Most are marketed in 6-inch pots, although production in 2¼-4-inch pots is expanding. Amortizing the cost of either size over several seasons, however, makes these plants lower priced than annuals. When perennials become crowded, division of roots is possible and other beds can be established.

Perennials are of relatively low maintenance. Although many people promoting perennials claim they are virtually maintenance free, this is not the case. However, they do fit into modern life styles. Gardeners want landscape beauty with relatively low labor output.

Expanding on this philosophy have been proponents of natural landscapes, where shrubs, wildflowers, bulbs and perennials are allowed to be wild. Such sites can be prairie or woodland, providing not only seasonal beauty, but food and cover for various forms of wildlife.

Whatever type of planting is chosen must be consistent with the gardener's goals, planting site and availability of suitable plant material. This should not be difficult with perennials. Cultural requirements and growth habits are diverse enough to meet nearly any need.

PERENNIAL BORDERS AND BEDS

Perennials' main use is in a well thought-out flower garden or bed that can provide beauty, fragrance, and flowers for cutting from spring until late autumn.

Positioning of these beds usually is best along the side or back of the home. Landscapers reserve the front or public side of a house for a more formal appearance, free from riotous color. Yet, where a long driveway leads to an estate sized lot or where there is opportunity for accent and specimen plantings, perennials can be used in good taste. Not taken into account are the ground-cover roles many perennials fulfill in the landscape, which are discussed later in this chapter.

Perennial borders have traditionally been long and narrow, usually backing up to a garage, fence or evergreen screen, thus providing a suitable backdrop for the succession of color to come from early spring until autumn. Suitable garden sites are easily viewed from living areas within the home.

Tying the garden to indoor living areas is a goal of professional landscapers today. For the border to be attractive, plants should be arranged in stairstep fashion so short plants are in front and taller varieties at the back. Flowers should be planted in groups because single rows will not achieve the visual effect desired.

Bloom color will also have an effect on bed appearance. A bed or border dominated by bright colors will appear much closer than one containing mostly cool tones. Combining bright and cool colored varieties within the same bed, therefore, becomes an art form to achieve visual harmony and provide continuing interest throughout the growing season.

Many variations of the traditional border have emerged in recent years. Perennials are being combined with flowering shrubs or dwarf conifers to become an integral part of the landscape plan. We also see the traditional perennial border becoming a haven for hardy bulbs, especially when early spring color is desired. Planting pockets for tender annuals are also being incorporated into perennial borders to help achieve a different look from spring until autumn. As early flowering varieties fade, plants are replaced by later flowering ones.

Relatively new are island beds and borders that are not placed against a screen or building. Both can be extremely attractive, primarily because plant performance is improved. Exposure to sunlight is more even and air circulation better. Island beds give a three dimensional effect and allow better viewing of plants selected. With these kinds of beds, tall plants are placed in the center, and dwarf kinds around the perimeter. The only problem with island beds is that they are hard to place in relation to other elements in the landscape. Professional landscapers usually want large uncluttered open spaces in the center of the planting scheme, although such a bed may be a suitable divider between play and work areas.

Regardless of what shape a perennial garden takes, it is wise to provide an edging to prevent the encroachment of lawn grasses and possible mechanical damage to flowers from lawn equipment. Such an edging will also give the bed form.

Flagstone, bonsai posts, railroad ties, landscape timbers or even plastic lawn edging can be used. Also remember that flagstones or decorative masonry blocks can be used to provide a pathway into the garden for maintenance and cutting purposes.

Winter months are usually the best time to begin planning a bed or border. By using graph paper, an outline of the bed can be traced and planting areas for each variety can be drawn to scale.

As you begin choosing varieties, consider your gardening goals. Do you wish a succession of bloom from early spring to late autumn? Is fragrance important? Do you want a wide variety of flowers present that can yield fresh or dried bouquets?

Once these goals are established, plants can then be selected according to:
1. Light and soil requirements.
2. Plant height.
3. Time and length of flowering period.
4. Flower color.

BED OR BORDER PREPARATION

Once planting decisions have been made, bed preparation becomes the most important task for the gardener.

This preparation begins with the thorough spading or tilling of the soil to at least 1 ft. Soil should be loose and well-draining. If it contains heavy clay, sand and peat should be worked in while spading so entry of air and water is eased. If the clay problem is serious, it may be necessary to insert drain tile to remove excess moisture or build up the bed's soil level to above grade to drain well.

Conversely, if soil is sandy and therefore too well-drained, peat and other organic materials should be added to help hold moisture before it escapes from the root zone.

While spading, it also is a good idea to work in an all-purpose garden fertilizer at the recommended rate. Then, apply broadleaf and grassy weedkillers and let the ground lie fallow for two weeks.

The garden is then ready to receive plants, although top dressing with an organic mulch following planting will help conserve moisture and discourage any late germinating weeds. Those that do appear can be easily pulled. Fertilizer should be lightly applied every two weeks during the growing season to maintain plant vigor.

These same steps should be taken before planting rock gardens and groundcovers, although a number of groundcovers tolerate too wet or droughty conditions without a change in soil structure being necessary.

ROCK GARDENS

The rock garden has long been a favorite way to display low-growing perennials and herbs. Not only can it make use of an otherwise little used hillside location, but when skillfully constructed, such a garden can give the appearance of a natural outcropping.

Although a hillside is the best terrain for establishing such a garden, a relatively flat area can be built up with soil and rock to form a berm. Shrubs and groundcover can be used to plant one side and the rock garden constructed on the other.

With either a natural or contrived location, rocks must be gathered that are in rough rectangular shape to construct terraces across the hillside. Terraces should be placed at irregular intervals. A more natural appearance is achieved if terraces do not go completely across the hillside. Width of terraces will depend on degree of slope desired. A good height between terraces is about 20 inches. Rocks should be buried up to one half of their height to achieve an outcropping appearance.

Soil used to backfill behind each terrace should be well-draining and relatively weed free. However, terracing can provide an opportunity to modify soil conditions for certain plants. Some rock garden plants may prefer a sandy or gravelly soil, while at the other end of the spectrum, a number of plants will do best in organic soils, high in leaf mold or peat. Because the planting area of each terrace is limited, it is fairly easy to provide a diversity of soil types.

Perennials most attractive in rock gardens are those that grow 12-15 inches. Some are upright growers, others are clump formers and many are creeping or trailing in habit. The most predominant group is made up of plants classified as Alpines, having originated above 3,200 feet in mountainous areas of the world. Yet, many worthwhile rock garden plants began their existence in other environments, with most having a similar need for well-drained soils and full sun.

Because of these needs, rock gardens should not be placed in deep shade. Plants should also be far enough away from shrubs or trees to avoid competition for available food and moisture.

Place plants in the rock garden according to their light and moisture needs, keeping those that like droughty conditions near the top of the slope, and moisture lovers near the bottom.

Some suggested plants for rock garden use are shown below. Cultural needs and illustrations of each are shown on pages 18 through 88.

Acaena microphylla
Achillea tomentosa
Aethionema 'Warley Rose'
Ajuga reptans
Alyssum saxatile (Aurinia saxatilis)
Anemone pulsatilla
Antennaria dioica
Arabis albida
Arenaria montana
Arenebia echioides
Artemisia schmidtiana 'Nana'
Aubrieta leichtlinii
Campanula carpatica
*Cerastium tomentosum**
*Ceratostigma plumbaginoides**
Cherianthus cheiri
Dianthus deltoides
Dianthus plumarius
Euphorbia myrsinites
Gentiana septemfida
Gypsophila repens
Helianthemum serphyllum
Iberis sempervirens
Leontopodium alpinum
Linum perenne
Liriope spicata
Papaver alpinum
Phlox subulata
Potentilla aurea

Primula auricula hyb.
Saponaria ocymoides
Sedum var.
Sempervivum var.
Teucrium chamaedrys nanum
Thymus citriodorus
Tunica saxifraga (Petrorhagia saxifraga)
Veronica prostrata

*Not suitable for confined areas.

ROCK GARDEN BUILDING

Hillside locations are best suited for rock gardens.

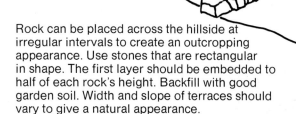

Rock can be placed across the hillside at irregular intervals to create an outcropping appearance. Use stones that are rectangular in shape. The first layer should be embedded to half of each rock's height. Backfill with good garden soil. Width and slope of terraces should vary to give a natural appearance.

PERENNIALS AS GROUNDCOVER

Low-growing, creeping or trailing perennials make many contributions to the home landscape as groundcover. Yet their primary functions are : (1) To tie elements of the landscape together into a harmonious composition; and (2) To stabilize soil in areas prone to erosion.

Landscape elements include trees, shrubs, buildings, fences, retaining walls, paved areas, and garden decor such as benches, statuary or lights. Although the most used groundcover for tying these elements together is grass, there are areas in the landscape where it should not be planted, either from a maintenance or visual standpoint.

For instance, a steep embankment may be nearly impossible to mow. Too much shade from nearby trees or shrubs may make grass impractical. On the other hand, dry sun-baked soils will not support grass without extensive modification. Grass also will do poorly in acidic, continually wet areas.

Meeting the demands of these problem areas can be done largely with perennial groundcovers. A list of plants that make good groundcovers is shown on page 16. Because of these plants' diverse cultural requirements, a suitable groundcover can be selected for nearly any situation.

There are areas within the landscape that naturally suit non-grass groundcovers. An example is the narrow strip of soil between a house and driveway. Another narrow area is near the foundation between shrubs or conifers.

If a groundcover is planted beneath a fence, stark lines of the fence are softened and the homeowner does not have the weekly chore of hand trimming grass around posts. Groundcovers also integrate statuary, benches and boulders into the landscape scene.

Groundcovers prevent soil erosion in two ways. Those with dense branching habits neutralize the force of raindrops, by breaking up each one into small droplets that soak into the soil rather than running off.

A number of other perennial groundcovers have underground stems that root as they spread, thereby binding the soil. These are ideal for embankment plantings. Depending on the degree of incline, it may be necessary, however, to insert artificial soil stabilizers such as rock or wood terraces across the slope to give plants a chance to become established.

Groundcover plants can also be planted to prevent mechanical damage to trees and shrubs from lawnmowers, sweepers or fertilizer spreaders. They also serve to modify the environment for neighboring plants. Well-known is the teaming of groundcovers with Clematis vines or Rhododendrons. Groundcovers provide the shade and moisture necessary to keep Clematis and Rhododendron roots cool. Other shallow rooted plants can be protected in the same manner.

Groundcovers also can modify the environment for man. Areas around the home that are sunbaked during much of the day can be planted to drought tolerant groundcovers, thereby decreasing soil surface temperatures. Transpiration of plant foliage cools the atmosphere.

In addition to perennials, there are three plant classes from which groundcovers can be chosen. These include shrubs, conifers and woody vines. Various combinations can be made with herbaceous perennial groundcovers for making attractive plantings. Some of the more popular conifers chosen for groundcover purposes are low-growing, spreading Junipers. These like plenty of sun and well-drained soils, making them ideal companions for perennials with similar needs.

Although some plants that we have listed in this book as perennials are actually woody vines or shrubs, many of these make useful groundcovers. English Ivy and its various cultivars create dense mats after several season's growth with foliage most years staying on the vine throughout winter months. Boston Ivy and its close relative Virginia Creeper also make good groundcover. Both have large glossy leaves that turn attractive shades of red and gold during autumn months.

One of the more widely used subshrubs is St. John's Wort, spreading by underground runners. Bright green foliage is topped by golden flowers throughout most of the growing season. There are a number of other spreading shrubs of deciduous or broadleaf evergreen habit that can be employed in home landscapes for their decorative and conservation purposes. Check with your local nurseryman regarding which varieties are suitable to your locale.

SPECIAL LOCALES

Although many special uses for perennials are discussed in this book, there are three areas that have not been mentioned.

The first of these is using perennials as specimen or accent plants within the landscape. Probably the most widely seen example is the combination of a tall shrubby perennial with some other landscape feature such as a fence, or its use in a planting containing a small tree, shrub and/or conifer. *Yucca filamentosa* and *Chrysanthemum maximum* are widely used in these combination plantings. Useful near conifers in foundation plantings or as a specimen near a fence is *Gypsophila paniculata*. In areas where perennial, a large clump of the decorative grass *Cortaderia selloana* makes a stately specimen planting.

Secondly, rock walls are being rediscovered as being suitable planting areas for creeping or trailing perennials. Tilted into the slope, these walls will last for many years without using mortar. Perennials can be planted in pockets between stones to add beauty and help stabilize embankment soil. Most plants of creeping or trailing habit listed for rock gardens can prove useful in rock walls. Because such walls are not solid, moisture can be released from the embankment without eroding soil or heaving during spring thaws.

Perennials also work well in containers, such as hanging baskets, patio pots and windowboxes. Obtain those varieties that are low to medium growing of upright or trailing habit.

Also select plants that bloom over a long season, so containers remain attractive during the time you enjoy your deck or patio. Perennials can be combined with annuals of early, mid season and late blooming habits to give a changing look throughout the growing season.

Perennials selected for container plantings should be those that tolerate well-drained soils, unless liberal amounts of water are applied. Moisture needs are greatest during hot dry periods with containers sometimes needing artifically applied moisture more than once a day.

Also, because the volume of soil is relatively small, plant roots expend nutrients more quickly than when placed in the garden. To keep plants looking their best, it will be necessary to begin a regular feeding program. However, because of fertilizer salt buildup over the course of the growing season, container perennials will need to be repotted the following spring to maintain their vigor.

...URE TOLERANT PERENNIALS

...gopodium variegatum (Sp-Su)
...quilegia hyb. (Su)
...renaria montana (Su)
...Aruncus sylvester (Su)
Baptisia australis (Su)
Bergenia cordifolia (Sp)
Brunnera macrophylla (Su)
Campanula persicifolia (Su)
Catananche caerulea (Su)
Centranthus ruber (Su)
Chrysanthemum morifolium (Su-F)
Digitalis purpurea (Su)
Doronicum caucasicum (Sp)
Epimedium niveum 'Alba' (Sp)
Filipendula hexapetala (Sp)
Gentiana septemfida (Su)
Geranium sanguineum (Su)
Hemerocallis hyb. (Su)
Heuchera sanguinea (Su)
Hosta hyb. (Su)
Iberis sempervirens (Sp)
Iris kaempferi (Su)
Iris sibirica (Su)
Liatris spicata (Su)
Liriope spicata (Su)
Lupinus hyb. (Su)
Lythrum hyb. (Su)
Mertensia virginica (Sp)
Monarda didyma (Su)
Nepeta mussinii (Sp-Su)
Oenothera missouriensis (Su)
Paeonia lactiflora (Sp)
Papaver orientalis (Su)
Phlox paniculata (Su)
Physostegia virginica (Su-F)
Polemonium hyb. (Sp)
Primula japonica (Sp)
Pulmonaria saccharata (Sp)
Tradescantia virginiana (Su)
Trollius ledebourii (Sp)

PERENNIALS BLOOMING SIX WEEKS OR LONGER

(Sp) = Spring flowering   (Su) = Summer flowering
(F) = Fall flowering

Achillea 'Coronation Gold' (Su)
Achillea filipendulina var. (Su)
Anaphalis triplinervis (Su-F)
Armeria maritima (Sp-Su)
Astilbe (Su)
Brunnera macrophylla (Sp-Su)
Campanula carpatica (Su-F)
Chrysanthemum morifolium var. (Su-F)
Chrysanthemum parthenium (Su)
Chrysanthemum virginianum (Su)
Cimcifuga racemosa (Su)
Coreopsis var. (Su)
Dicentra spectabilis (Sp)
Echinacea purpurea (Su-F)
Geranium sanguineum prostratum (Sp-Su)
Heliopsis cultivars (Su-F)
Lysimachia clethroides (Su)
Lythrum salicaria cultivars (Su)
Monarda didyma cultivars (Su)
Phlox paniculata var. (Su)
Platycodon grandiflora (Su)
Polygonum reynoutria (Su-F)
Rudbeckia fulgida 'Goldsturm' (Su-F)
Salvia nemerosa 'Superba' (Su-F)
Sedum spectabile cultivars (Su-F)

PERENNIALS FOR HOT, DRY SOILS

(Sp) = Spring flowering   (Su) = Summer flowering
(F) = Fall flowering   (I) = Fall flowering

Hot, sunbaked soils are difficult places to plant. However, perennials on the following list can tolerate such conditions.

Acaena microphylla (Su)
Achillea tomentosa & hyb. (Su)
Anaphalis triplinervis (Su)
Anthemis tinctoria (Su-F)
Arabis alpina (Sp)
Artemisia schmidtiana 'Nana' (I)
Asclepias tuberosa (Su)
Alyssum saxatilis (Sp)
Campanula persicifolia (Su)
Catananche caerulea (Su)
Cerastium tomentosum (Su)
Cheiranthus cheiri (Sp)
Coreopsis hyb. (Su)
Dianthus plumarius (Su)
Echinacea purpurea (Su-F)
Echinops hyb. (Su-F)
Eryngium amethystinum (Su)
Euphorbia myrsinites (Su)
Euphorbia polychroma (Su)
Gaillardia aristata (Su-F)
Gypsophila paniculata (Su)
Helianthemum serphyllum (Su)
Hemerocallis hyb. (Su)
Iberis sempervirens (Sp)
Kniphofia uvaria (Su)
Lavandula angustifolia (Su)
Liatris spicata (Su-F)
Linum perenne (Su)
Lychnis chalcedonica (Su)
Penstemon heterophyllus (Su)
Potentilla aurea (Su)
Salvia virgata nemerosa (Su)
Santolina chamaecyparisus (Su)
Sedum hyb. (Su-F)
Sempervivum hyb. (Su)
Stachys lanata (Su)
Thymus vulgaris (Sp)
Tunica saxifraga (Su)
Veronica incana (Su)
Yucca sp. (Su)

PERENNIALS THAT CUT WELL

(Sp) = Spring flowering   (Su) = Summer flowering
(F) = Fall flowering

Perennial gardening satisfaction is increased by bringing frequent bouquets of flowers into the home. If flowers are cut often, plants increase production and bloom over a longer period. A number also work well in dried bouquets. These are shown with an (*). Dried perennials can be combined with wildflowers, ornamental grasses and shrubs with interesting branching habits to make attractive autumn arrangements.

*Achillea 'Coronation Gold' (Su)
*Achillea tomentosum (Su)
 Alcea rosea (Su-F)
 Alchemilla mollis
 Anthemis tinctoria (Su-F)
 Aquilegia 'McKana Hybrids' (Sp)
 Aster hyb. (Su-F)
 Astilbe hyb. (Su)
 Campanula carpatica (Su-F)
 Campanula persicifolia (Su)
*Catananche caerulea (Su)
 Centaurea dealbata (Su-F)
 Centranthus ruber (Su-F)
 Chrysanthemum coccineum (Su-F)
 Chrysanthemum morifolium (Su-F)
 Chrysanthemum maximum (Su-F)

Coreopsis verticillata (Su-F)
Delphinium hyb. (Sp-Su)
Dianthus barbatus (Sp)
Dianthus caryophyllus (Sp)
Dicentra spectabilis (Sp)
Doronicum caucasicum (Sp)
*Echinacea purpurea (Su-F)
*Echinops hyb. (Su-F)
Erigeron speciosa (Su)
Gaillardia aristata (Su-F)
Geum borisii (Sp-Su)
*Gypsophila paniculata (Su)
Helenium hyb. (Su-F)
Helianthus multiflorus (Su)
Heliopsis scabra incomparabilis (Su-F)
Heuchera sanguinea (Sp-Su-F)
Hosta hyb. (Su)
Kniphofia uvaria (Su-F)
Liatris spicata (Su-F)
Lupinus 'Russell Hybrids' (Sp-Su)
Lychnis chalcedonica (Su)
Lysimachia clethroides (Su)
Lythrum 'Morden's Pink' (Su)
Monarda didyma (Su)
Myosotis scorpioides semperflorens (Sp-Su-F)
Paeonia lactiflora (Sp)
*Physalis franchetti (Su)
Physostegia virginica (Su-F)
Rudbeckia fulgida (Su-F)
Scabiosa caucasica (Su-F)
*Sedum spectabile hyb. (Su-F)
*Solidolgo hyb. (Su-F)
Stokesia laevis (Su-F)
Thalictrum aquilegifolium (Sp-Su)
Veronica, tall cult. & hyb. (Su)

PERENNIALS THAT MAKE GOOD GROUNDCOVERS

(Sp) = Spring flowering   (Su) = Summer flowering
(F) = Fall flowering   (I) = Flowers Insignificant

A number of perennials make good groundcovers. The following list includes only those that have a wide hardiness range and are relatively easy to maintain.

Achillea tomentosa (Su)
Aegopodium variegatum (Su)
Ajuga reptans (Sp)
Alchemilla mollis (Su)
Arabis albida (Sp)
Arenaria verna (Sp-Su)
Armeria maritima (Sp-Su)
Artemisia schmidtiana 'Nana' (I)
Asperula odorata (Sp-Su)
Bergenia cordifolia (Sp)
Cerastium tomentosum (Sp-Su)
Ceratostigma plumbaginoides (Su-F)
Chrysogonum virginianum
Convallaria majalis (Sp)
Coronilla varia (Sp-Su-F)
Dianthus deltoides (Sp)
Euonymus fortunei coloratus (I)
Festuca ovina glauca (I)
Iberis sempervirens (Sp)
Lamium maculatum (Sp)
Lysimachia nummularia (Su)
Myosotis scorpioides semperflorens (Sp-Su)
Nepeta mussinii (Su-F)
Ophiopogon japonicus (Su)
Pachysandra terminalis (Sp)
Phlox subulata (Sp)
Polygonum reynoutria (Su-F)
Potentilla aurea (Su)
Sedum hyb. (Su)
Stachys lanata (Su)

Thymus serphyllum (Su)
Veronica incana (Su)
Vinca minor (Sp)

PERENNIALS THAT PROVIDE GARDEN FRAGRANCE

(Sp) = Spring flowering   (Su) = Summer flowering
(F) = Fall flowering

Perennials that provide fragrance as well as beauty can greatly enhance gardening pleasure. An attempt should be made to place these plants where they can be enjoyed; near walkways, as border edging, or in patio containers. Foliage as well as flowers can provide a pleasing aroma. Plants with aromatic foliage are included with an (*).

*Achillea tomentosa (Su)
*Artemisia lactiflora (Su)
 Artemisia stellerana (Su)
 Aubrieta leichtlinii (Sp)
 Centranthus ruber (Su-F)
*Chrysanthemum morifolium (Su-F)
 Clematis, hyb. (Su)
 Convallaria majalis (Sp)
 Delphinium hyb. (Sp)
 Dianthus barbatus (Su)
 Dianthus caryophyllus (Su)
 Dictamnus alba (Su)
 Filipendula hexapetala (Sp)
 Hemerocallis hyb. (Su)
 Hosta plantaginea hyb. (Su)
 Hyssopus officinalis (Su)
 Incarvillea delavayi (Sp)
 Iris X germanica hyb. (Sp)
 Lavandula angustifolia (Su)
 Lupinus 'Russell Hybrids' (Su)
 Lythrum hyb. (Su)
 Matricaria capensis (Sp)
*Monarda didyma (Su)
*Nepeta mussinii (Sp)
 Paeonia lactiflora (Sp)
 Phlox paniculata (Su)
 Primula vulgaris (Sp)
*Ruta graveolens (Su)
*Santolina chamaecyparissus (Su)
 Thymus vulgaris (Su)

PERENNIALS THAT TOLERATE DRY SHADE

(Sp) = Spring flowering   (Su) = Summer flowering
(F) = Fall flowering

Dry shaded areas are often the most difficult to plant. Not only do plants suffer from lack of sunlight, but available moisture is exhausted by neighboring trees and shrubs. To overcome such conditions, it is a good idea to add large amounts of organic mulch and begin regular watering and feeding programs because such soils are not only water deficient, but also depleted in plant nutrients.

Alchemilla mollis (Su)
Anaphalis triplinervis
Brunnera macrophylla (Su)
Epimedium niveum (Sp)
Geranium hyb. (Su)
Lamium maculatum hyb. (Sp)
Pachysandra terminalis (Sp)
Polygonatum commutatum (Sp-Su)
Polygonum affine (F)
Pulmonaria saccharata (Sp)
Stachys lanata (Su)
Vinca minor (Sp)

A SUMMER BORDER FEATURING, FROM FRONT TO BACK, RED FLOWERING DIANTHUS BARBATUS, YELLOW CORE-OPSIS, SILVER FOLIAGED SANTOLINA CHAMAECYPARIS, WHITE IBERIS SEMPERVIRENS, BLUE SPIKED BAPTISIA AUSTRALIS, WOOLY WHITE STACHYS LANATA AND PINK MONARDA DIDYMA 'CROFTWAY PINK'.

GUIDE TO COMMERCIAL PERENNIAL VARIETIES

As stated above, perennial varieties shown on the following 72 pages are in wide cultivation. Our purpose is to acquaint gardeners, landscape specifiers and retail merchandisers with perennials that are generally available from growers nationwide.

To make this section useful on a day to day basis, listings are in alphabetical order by botanical name. Common names are shown in parentheses and an effort has also been made to research popular cultivars.

Included is a series of symbols to quickly identify plant traits and light needs. These symbols are:

○ = **Full Sun**   〰 = **Ground Cover**

◑ = **Partial Shade**   ♠ = **Evergreen**

● = **Full Shade**   ✕ = **Cut Flower**

A cross reference index on pages 96-97 can also assist the reader with plant selection.

NEW ZEALAND BUR

SOFT ACANTHUS or BEARS BREECH

FERN-LEAVED YARROW

ACAENA MICROPHYLLA ○▲✂
(New Zealand Bur)

Evergreen trailing plant useful for rock gardens in protected areas. Produces deep red burrs from early to late summer. Leaves are bronze-green.
Hardy Zones: 6-9.
Grows: 6-8" (15-20cm).
Culture: Does best in well-drained garden soils. Needs a straw mulch in winter.
Spacing: 12-15" (30-38cm).

ACANTHUS MOLLIS ○◑
(Soft Acanthus or Bear's Breech)

Although this plant is perennial in Zones 8-10, it is best grown for unusual tropical looking foliage north of Zone 8, where it can be attractive in patio pots and urns. Where allowed to take root in the garden, spikes of rose, pink, lilac or white flowers are produced in August. Is invasive if roots are allowed to spread.
Hardy Zones: 8-10.
Grows: 18-24" (45-60cm).
Culture: Does well in ordinary well-drained garden soil.

Spacing: 36" (90cm).

ACHILLEA FILIPENDULINA 'CORONATION GOLD' ○✂
(Fern-Leaved Yarrow)

Probably the best known of Fern-Leaved Yarrow, Coronation Gold produces flat heads of golden yellow flowers throughout the summer. Foliage has a soft ferny texture and emits a pungent odor. Excellent variety for the back of the border or wildflower garden. Excellent plant for dried arrangements.
Hardy Zones: 3-10.
Grows: 40-48" (1-1.2m).
Culture: Does best in well-drained soils. Can tolerate droughty conditions.
Spacing: 24" (60cm).

ACHILLEA MILLEFOLIUM ROSEUM ○✂
(Common Yarrow)

Modern varieties trace their ancestry to ivory colored wildflowers of northern Europe. Most popular in this country are rose or magenta-red hybrids bearing flat-

COMMON YARROW

SNEEZEWORT

WOOLLY YARROW

headed blooms from midsummer until fall. These produce ferny foliage. *A. m. 'Red Beauty',* shown above, is widely grown.

Hardy Zones: 3-10.
Grows: 18" (45cm).
Culture: Does best in well-drained soils. Can tolerate droughty conditions.
Spacing: 15" (38cm).

ACHILLEA PTARMICA ○✂
(Sneezewort)

Outstanding perennial for the border or cutting. So named because its roots were once used for making snuff. Ball-shaped blooms are produced during summer months above willowlike foliage. Flowers are white and grow in clusters.

Hardy Zones: 3-10.
Grows: 15-25" (38-62cm).
Culture: Does best in well-drained soils. Tolerates droughty conditions.
Spacing: 12-15" (30-38cm).

ACHILLEA TOMENTOSA ○✂
(Woolly Yarrow)

Creeping mat-forming variety producing gray-green foliage above which sulphur-yellow flowers are displayed from early summer until early autumn. Several kinds are available, varying primarily in shade of yellow blooms produced on mature height.

Hardy Zones: 3-10.
Grows: 6-12" (15-30cm).
Culture: Does best in well-drained soils. Tolerates droughty conditions.
Spacing: 15-18" (38-45cm).

AZURE MONKSHOOD

WARLEY ROSE CANDYTUFT

SILVEREDGE BISHOPS WEED

ACONITUM ACONITUM ◐●✂
(Monkshood)
One of several popular Monkshood forms, bearing amethyst-blue flowers on robust plants usually grown at the back of the perennial border. Flowers appear in mid-summer. Foliage is deeply cut and glossy, making a good background to shorter perennials in the garden.
Hardy Zones: 3-8.
Grows: 48-60" (1.2-1.5m)
Culture: Does best in moist soils high in organic matter.
Spacing: 12-18" (30-45cm).

ADENOPHORA CONFUSA ○
(Ladybells)
Reliable perennial often confused with Canterbury Bells producing deep blue flowers on tall spikes in midsummer.
Hardy Zones: 4-8.
Grows: 36" (90cm).
Culture: Does best in moist soils.
Spacing: 18-24" (45-60cm).

ADONIS AMURENSIS and *A. VERNALIS* ○◐
(Amur Adonis and Spring Adonis)

These low growing perennials appear soon after frost leaves the ground, producing bright flowers of yellow, pink, white, orange and copper over a long blooming period. Foliage is feathery and flowers are borne 2-3 per stem. Spring Adonis has the wider color range. The buttercup like blooms of Amur Adonis appear only in yellow and white. Both are good foreground plants for the perennial bed or border.
Hardy Zones: 3-7.
Grows: 12-15" (30-38cm).
Culture: Does well in nearly any well drained garden soil.
Spacing: 6-10" (15-25cm).

AEGOPODIUM PODOGRARIA VARIEGATUM ○◐●✂
(Silveredge Bishops Weed)
Fast-growing groundcover producing attractive green leaves with silver margins. Clusters of small white flowers are produced in midsummer. Good for difficult areas, such as under trees, where little else will grow.
Hardy Zones: 3-10.
Grows: 10-15" (25-38cm).
Culture: Not particular to location, doing well in dry to

BUGLE

BUGLEWEED

BRONZE BEAUTY BUGLE

moist soils.
Spacing: 6-12" (15-30cm).

AETHIONEMA 'WARLEY ROSE' ○▲
(Persian Candytuft or Persian Stonecress)
Compact-growing, shrubby plant with blue-green needle-like leaves borne year-round. Warley Rose produces bright pink flowers in April and May. Good plant for rock gardens or near the front of a perennial border.
Hardy Zones: 6-9.
Grows: 6-8" (15-20cm).
Culture: Does best in well-drained soil.
Spacing: 12-15" (30-38cm).

AJUGA GENEVENSIS
and *A. REPTANS VAR.* ○◑●₩▲
(Bugle)
Ajuga makes a neat groundcover, spreading rapidly and producing large shiny leaves in various colors. Flowers are produced in early spring in blue or pink. *A. genevensis* is of somewhat looser habit than *A. reptans* varieties. It produces green leaves or green with silver margins. Popular *A. reptans* varieties are Bronze Beauty,

Metallica Crispa and Burgundy Glow. Metallica Crispa has deep bronze-purple foliage, Bronze Beauty, a distinct bronze color, and Burgundy Glow bronze with a wine-red cast. All do well in sun or light shade, but leaf colors are enhanced in more exposed locations and as foliage matures during the growing season.
Hardy Zones: 4-10.
Grows: 6-8" (15-20cm).
Culture: Does well in nearly any garden soil that does not dry out easily.
Spacing: 6-12" (15-30cm).

AJUGA PYRAMIDALIS ○◑₩▲
(Bugleweed)
Contrary to other Ajuga, this form does not spread. It is a clump former, sending up blue flowers on 10" (25cm) spikes in spring. Because of its reliable attractive flowering habit, the plant makes a worthy addition to the flower border, particularly where soil is moist.
Hardy Zones: 4-10.
Grows: 10" (25cm).
Culture: Does best in moist soil high in organic matter.
Spacing: 8-10" (20-25cm).

PERENNIAL HOLLYHOCKS

LADY'S MANTLE

DECORATIVE ONIONS or CHIVES

ALCEA ROSEA ○
(Perennial Hollyhocks)

Perennial Hollyhocks produce large blooms on tall stalks throughout summer months. Blooms are either single, ruffled, frilled, or double and span nearly every shade of white, pink, red, yellow or lavender. Blooms are produced in clusters, starting 18″ (45cm) from the top of each stalk, proceeding upward. Because of their height, Perennial Hollyhocks look best in the back of the perennial border or against a fence.
Hardy Zones: 3-8.
Grows: 60-96″ (1.5-2.4m).
Culture: Does well in moist, but well-drained garden soil. Where windy, stalks may need staking.
Spacing: 15-18″ (38-45cm).

ALCHEMILLA VULGARIS ◑
(Lady's Mantle)

Lady's Mantle is a low maintenance perennial producing large gray-green fan-shaped leaves, above which appear dainty yellow flowers in May and June. Because the plant spreads by means of seed produced by spent blooms, it becomes invasive in limited areas if flower heads are not removed soon after wilting. Good groundcover for no traffic areas.
Hardy Zones: 3-10.
Grows: 18″ (45cm).
Culture: Does best in moist, but well-drained soil.
Spacing: 10-12″ (25-30cm).

ALLIUM SENESCENS & A. S. GLAUCUM ○ ◑
(Decorative Onions or Chives)

Although these two forms of Chives are primarily used in the rock garden, probably their most attractive use is as border edging. Both forms bloom in summer, although *A. senescens* produces rose-pink flowers in June while *A. s. glaucum* lilac blooms in August. Most compact at 4-8″ (10-20cm) is *A. senescens. A. s. glaucum* grows to 12″ (30cm). The edible form, *A. schoenoprasum* is described elsewhere in this book.
Hardy Zones: 4-9.
Grows: 4-12″ (10-30cm).
Culture: Does best in well-drained soil.
Spacing: 4-6″ (10-15cm).

BORDER SCENE COMPOSED OF, FRONT TO BACK, CORONATION GOLD YARROW, SWEET WILLIAM AND DELPHINIUM.

BASKET-OF-GOLD

ALYSSUM SAXATILE and *A. MONTANUM* ○ ◑ ⋈
(Basket of Gold)

These spreading perennials are spectacular when completely covered with bright to golden yellow single or double flowers from mid to late spring. Gray-green foliage makes a good background to flowers, yet provides garden interest when the plants are not in bloom. Both Basket of Gold forms are widely used in rock gardens and are especially attractive when allowed to cascade over boulders and rock walls. *A. montanum* is more compact growing, however, and better suited to confined planting areas. Reclassified in recent years, *A. saxatile* may also be found under the name *Aurinia saxatilis,* although growers prefer the old name for marketing reasons.

Hardy Zones: 4-9.
Grows: 8-12" (20-30cm).
Culture: Does best in well-drained garden soils.
Spacing: 12" (30cm).

AMSONIA TABERNAEMONTANA ◑
(Milkweed)

Low maintenance perennial with pale blue foliage. Ideal for planting in natural settings or near shrubbery. Blooms

DWARF BASKET OF GOLD

PEARLY EVERLASTING

MILKWEED

ALKANET

in May and June.
Hardy Zones: 3-9.
Grows: 36" (90cm).
Culture: Does well in nearly any garden soil.
Spacing: 15-18" (38-45cm).

ANAPHALIS TRIPLINERVIS ○✄
(Pearly Everlasting)

Compact-growing perennial producing flat clusters of white flowers buttonlike in appearance. Foliage is slender and covered with white hairs. Good plant for front of the floral border or in the rock garden. As the name implies, it is a good cut flower that can also be used for dried arrangements. A more growthy version is *A. yedoensis* or Japanese Pearly Everlasting. Both kinds bloom from midsummer to autumn.
Hardy Zones: 3-6.
Grows: 12-24" (30-60cm).
Culture: Does well in nearly any well-drained garden soil and tolerates dry conditions.
Spacing: 12-15" (30-38cm).

ANCHUSA AZUREA ○
(Alkanet or Italian Bugloss)

These are the old-fashioned Forget-Me-Nots that grandma used to grow. Small star-shaped flowers of varying blue shades are produced in clusters during May and June on tall bushy stems clothed with large tongue shaped deep green leaves. Alkanet is easy to grow. Because of its bushy habit, this perennial makes a good border flower. Although some varieties grow 5-6 ft. (150-180cm.), ones most popular stay within the height range shown below.
Hardy Zones: 5-10.
Grows: 18-36" (45-90cm).
Culture: Does best in well-drained soil.
Spacing: 18-24" (45-60cm).

25

JAPANESE ANEMONE

ANEMONE JAPONICA ○◑✄
(Japanese Anemone or Windflower)

These attractive perennials provide late summer color when little else is in bloom. Pink or white, single or double, flowers are produced on tall wiry stems in August and September. Foliage is light green and deeply lobed. Japanese Anemones are best placed near the back of a perennial border because of their height.

Hardy Zones: 6-10.
Grows: 30-36" (75-90cm).
Culture: Does best in moist, but well-drained soils high in organic matter.
Spacing: 18" (45cm).

ANEMONE PULSATILLA ○◑
(Pasque Flower)

This compact-growing perennial produces bell-shaped violet-purple flowers in April. Tiny ornamental ferny leaves follow flower production. Blooms are replaced by globe-shaped masses of silvery down in late summer. White and red flowering varieties are available. This is a good plant near the front of a border or in the rock garden.

Hardy Zones: 4-9.
Grows: 8-10" (20-25cm).
Culture: Does best in well-drained soil.
Spacing: 10-12" (25-30cm).

ANEMONE VITIFOLIA ROBUSTISSIMA ◑
(Grape-Leaved Anemone)

Attractive hardy perennial producing rose pink blooms on wiry stems from late summer into autumn. Grape like deep green foliage is produced in a low mound at the plant's base, above which flowers rise 2-3 ft. Plants should be placed in the garden or border where they can remain undisturbed for a number of years.

Hardy Zones: 5-10.
Grows: 2-3 ft. (60-90cm).
Culture: Does best in well drained, but moist soils high in organic matter. Needs a winter mulch of straw or hay in Zones 5-6.
Spacing: 18" (45cm).

KELWAY GOLDEN MARGUERITE (Detail)

PASQUE FLOWER

KELWAY GOLDEN MARGUERITE

PUSSYTOES

ANTENNARIA DIOICA & A. TOMENTOSA ○ ⋙
(Pussytoes)

These are low-growing mat formers useful both as groundcovers in the rock garden or between flagstones. *A. dioica* produces silvery foliage and rose-pink flowers in June. At 3-4" (7.5-10cm) it is the more compact growing. *A. tomentosa* grows 12" (30cm) and produces silver leaves. White flowers are produced in June.
Hardy Zones: 3-9.
Grows: 3-12" (7.5-30cm).
Culture: Thrives in infertile soil.
Spacing: 10-12" (25-30cm).

ANTHEMIS TINCTORIA 'KELWAYI' & A. BIEBERSTEINIANA ○ ▲ ✕
(Golden Marguerite)

Golden Marguerites are showy perennials producing attractive daisy-like flowers of yellow or gold from summer until early autumn. *A. t. 'Kelwayi'* exhibits dark green finely cut foliage. Plants are vigorous, growing 30"

(75cm), with equal spread. Of similar habit is the orange flowering Beauty of Grallagh. *A. biebersteiniana* is a dwarf, producing flowers with buttonlike centers from early summer until autumn and silvery finely cut foliage. Another low grower is E.C. Buxton, one of few white varieties. Sparkling daisylike blooms have golden centers.
Hardy Zones: 3-9.
Grows: Dwarf: 10-12" (25-30cm). Standard: 24-30" (60-75cm).
Culture: Does well in nearly any well-drained garden soil.
Spacing: 12-24" (30-60cm).

AQUILEGIA HYBRIDS ○ ◑ ✕
(Columbine)

Columbines are attractive perennials for the flower border, producing star-shaped flowers with long spurs in a wide range of pastel blue, pink, red, lavender, yellow and white colors from mid to late spring. Popular full size series are McKana and Spring Song. Biedermeier is a mid size series and Dragon Fly is the best known dwarf strain. In all cases, flowers are produced above neat

COLUMBINE

ROCK CRESS

clumps of deep green or blue-green airy foliage. All are good cut flowers.
Hardy Zones: 3-10.
Grows: 18-36" (45-90cm).
Culture: Does best in well-drained soils.
Spacing: 10-15" (25-38cm).

ARABIS ALPINA and *A. CAUCASICA VAR.* ○ ▲✂
(Rock Cress)

Rock Cress is a creeping perennial useful for rock gardens and edging. Flowers are pink or white, double or single, depending on variety. Snow Cap is a pure white *A. alpina* variety producing blooms that cover the plant in spring. Spring Charm, however, is a member of the *A. caucasica* group, producing pink flowers above soft gray-green foliage. Both spread rapidly, each plant capable of covering an 18" diameter.
Hardy Zones: 3-10.
Grows: 4-6" (10-15cm).
Culture: Does best in well-drained soils.
Spacing: 12-15" (30-38cm).

ARENARIA MONTANA & *A. VERNA CAESPITOSA VAR.* ○ ◑ ⌇▲
(Sandwort)

A. montana is a creeping perennial with moss-like foliage above which are produced white flowers in early summer. Similar, but not as tall, is *A. caespitosa,* producing white star-shaped flowers in May. Both are excellent plants for between flagstones and in rock gardens.
Hardy Zones: 4-9.
Grows: 3-5" (7.5-12cm).
Culture: Does best in well-drained soils of low fertility.
Spacing: 10-12" (25-30cm).

ARMERIA MARITIMA ○ ⌇▲
(Sea Pink)

Sea Pink is a reliable perennial producing grasslike semi-evergreen foliage and globe-shaped clusters of tiny white, pink or rose-red flowers. Blooming period is early summer, although additional flowers are produced later in the season where summers are cool. When not in bloom, the foliage makes interesting groundcover that

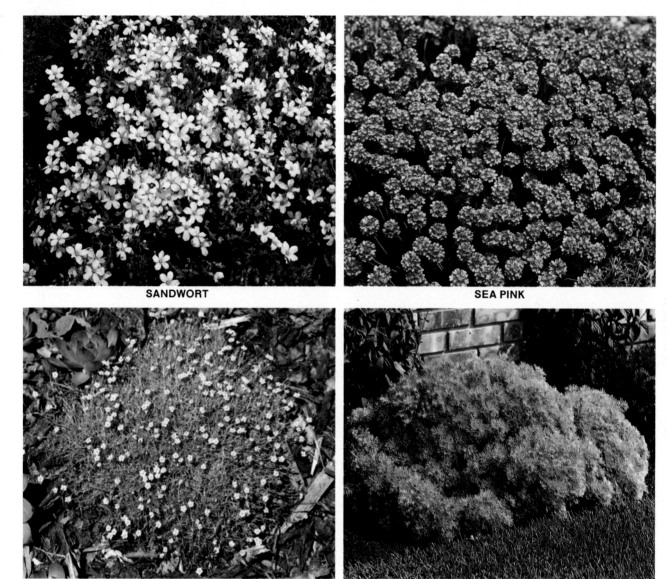

SANDWORT

SEA PINK

IRISH MOSS

SILVER MOUND

is attractive in beds, rock gardens and near walkways.
Hardy Zones: 2-10.
Grows: 10-12″ (25-30cm).
Culture: Does best in well-drained, sandy soils.
Spacing: 12″ (30cm).

ARTEMISIA SCHMIDTIANA ○ ◐
(Silver Mound)

Silver Mound is a low-growing, dome-shaped perennial featuring silvery gray foliage. Plants are attractive in the rock garden or as edging. Tiny clusters of flowers appear in late summer, which can be removed to maintain the 'mound' shape.
Hardy Zones: 3-10.
Grows: 12″ (30cm).
Culture: Does best in well-drained soil.
Spacing: 12-15″ (30-38cm).

ARTEMISIA LUDOVICIANA 'SILVER KING' ○ ◐
(White Sage)

Prized for its frosty silver foliage. White Sage is an attrac-

tive accent plant, providing a pleasing contrast to green and blue foliage colors of other plants. Foliage is fragrant and widely used for making wreaths, floral arrangements and bouquets.
Hardy Zones: 5-9.
Grows: 24-30″ (60-75cm).
Culture: Does best in well-drained soil.
Spacing: 12-15″ (30-38cm).

ARTEMISIA DRACUNCULUS ○ ◐
(Tarragon)

Tarragon is a perennial herb with aromatic gray-green leaves that are also used to season chicken, fish, soups and salads. This upright-growing plant is also useful in the flower border, providing a pleasant background to low-growing plants.
Hardy Zones: 5-9.
Grows: 18″ (45cm).
Culture: Does best in well-drained soil.
Spacing: 12-15″ (30-38cm).

OLD WOMAN SAGE

BUTTERFLY FLOWER

GOATSBEARD

ARTEMISIA STELLERANA ○ ◐
(Old Woman Sage)

Typical of most sages, Old Woman Sage grows 24-30"
(60-75cm). It produces aromatic filigreed frosted foliage.
Yellow flowers are produced during summer months. This
plant is a good accent in the flower border. A dwarf
form is also available, however, that is attractive in rock
gardens and as border edging.
Hardy Zones: 4-10.
Grows: Standard: 24-30" (60-75cm). Dwarf: 6" (15cm).
Culture: Does best in well-drained soils.
Spacing: Standard 15-18" (38-45cm). Dwarf: 6-8"
(15-20cm).

ARUNCUS SYLVESTER ○ ◐
(Goatsbeard)

Goatsbeard is a tall perennial producing large plumes
of tiny ivory-white flowers in early summer. Foliage is
rich green and heavily veined. The plant is attractive
near the back of a perennial border or in mass plantings.
Hardy Zones: 4-9.
Grows: 48-72" (1.2-1.8m).
Culture: Does well in nearly any garden soil, including

those that remain wet for extended periods.
Spacing: 18-24" (45-60cm).

ASCLEPIAS TUBEROSA ○✂
(Butterfly Flower)

This reliable perennial produces 12-24" (30-60cm) stalks
topped by clusters of fragrant orange flowers from midsummer to early autumn. Flowers make excellent fresh
bouquets. Foliage is narrow and covered with minute
hair. Blooms are followed in autumn by canoe-shaped
seed pods that send forth silky seeds. Pods are widely
used in dried arrangements.
Hardy Zones: 4-10.
Grows: 12-24" (30-60cm).
Culture: Does best in well-drained, sandy soil.
Spacing: 10-12" (25-30cm).

ASPERULA ODORATA ○✂
(Sweet Woodruff)

This low-growing, mound-shaped perennial is often used
as a groundcover in rock gardens or areas where there is
light shade. Small white flowers adorn the plant in late

30

JENNY NEW YORK ASTER

SNOW CUSHION NEW YORK ASTER

HARRINGTON'S PINK NEW ENGLAND ASTER

spring and early summer. This perennial is commonly regarded as an herb because foliage is used dried in sachets. Flowers are fragrant and can be pleasing in the garden or when cut and brought indoors. (See reference to this useful plant in Perennial Herb section, page 96).
Hardy Zones: 4-9.
Grows: 8-10" (20-25cm).
Culture: Does best in moist, acidic soil high in organic matter.
Spacing: 12" (30cm).

ASTER NOVAE-ANGLIAE & A. NOVI-BELGII ○
(Michaelmas Daisy)

Although Michaelmas Daisy is the common name to describe *A. novae-angliae* and *A. novi-belgii* varieties, *A. novae-angliae* is also known as New England Aster and *A. novi-belgii*, as New York Aster. Both are noted for their reliability and long blooming season. Blooms within the two groups are typically single or double petaled and have golden centers. Standard varieties grow 36-48" (90-120cm). *A. novae-angliae* exhibits purple, pink or ruby-red flowers from late summer until autumn. Popular varieties include Harrington's Pink, September Ruby, and

Treasurer. The varieties making up *A. novi-belgii* are divided into standard and dwarf sizes. Hybridizers of *A. novi-belgii* varieties, in large and dwarf sizes, have increased the color range to include shades of blue, violet, red, pink and white. Like *A. novae-angliae,* the tall varieties are attractive near the back of the perennial border or in a wildgarden situation. The dwarfs, however, find best use in small beds or near the front of a border. These, like the standards, produce heavy late season color from August to October. Among the standard varieties, some of the more widely planted include Crimson Brocade with double red flowers; Eventide, a semi double violet-blue; and Mt. Everest, a pure white single. Widely planted dwarfs include Jenny, a double violet-blue; Professor Kippenberg, clear blue single; and Winston Churchill, a single red noted for its early flowering habit.

Hardy Zones: 4-8.
Grows: Dwarfs: 12-15" (30-38cm). Standards: 36-48" (90-120cm).
Culture: Does best in well-drained garden soils.
Spacing: Dwarfs: 12-15" (30-38cm). Standards: 18-24" (45-60cm).

31

CRIMSON BROCADE MICHAELMAS DAISY

WONDER OF STAFFA

PROFESSOR KIPPENBERG MICHAELMAS DAISY

ALPINE ASTER

ASTER ALPINUS ○ ◖
(Alpine Aster)

The Alpine Aster is a low-growing clump former producing bright or dark blue daisy-like flowers in summer. It is an excellent plant for rock gardens or as edging for a perennial border. Related is *A. alpellus,* also having *A. amellus* heritage. At 12" (30cm), this plant is 2-4" (5-10cm) taller than *A. alpina.* The most popular variety of *A. alpellus* is Triumph, producing violet-blue daisy flowers with copper centers, rather than gold. It also is an excellent rock garden and perennial border plant. Both flower from midsummer until late autumn.

Hardy Zones: 2-9.
Grows: 6-12" (15-30cm).
Culture: Does best in well-drained garden soil.
Spacing: 10-12" (25-30cm).

ASTER FRIKARTII ○ ◖ ✂
(Wonder of Staffa)

Wonder of Staffa is an Aster hybrid of medium height, producing lavender-blue daisylike blooms with golden centers. The plant is noted for its long season of bloom, often producing flowers from early June until frost. In mild areas, the plant blooms year-round. Like other tall asters, *A. frikartii* tends to be weak unless pruned twice during the growing season to stimulate branching. Prune stalks early in spring, then again a month later. Although blooms are among the largest of perennial asters, the plant is not as hardy as other tall forms such as *A. novae-angliae* and *A. novi-belgii.*

Hardy Zones: 6-9.
Grows: 18-24" (45-60cm).
Culture: Does best in well-drained garden soil.
Spacing: 15-18" (38-45cm).

ASTER YUNNANENSIS ○ ✂
(Napsbury Aster)

This native of China is a perennial of medium height producing bright blue flowers with orange centers. Petals are broader than *Aster frikartii* and bloom diameter is larger. Napsbury Aster is one of the few blooming from late spring to early summer. Each stem bears a solitary bloom and foliage is produced in a clump near the plant's base. This is another good border perennial that can be

BRIDAL VEIL ASTILBE

RHEINLAND ASTILBE

RED SENTINEL ASTILBE

used as a cut flower.
Hardy Zones: 5-10.
Grows: 24-30" (60-75cm).
Culture: Does best in moist, but well-drained garden soil.
Spacing: 15-18" (38-45cm).

ASTILBE ARENDSII ○ ◐ ✂
(Astilbe or False Spirea)

Astilbe is one of the best perennials for brightening a dark corner of the flower border. It produces spires of tiny white, pink or red flowers during midsummer. Foliage is ferny, varying in color from bronze to dark green. If florets are allowed to open fully, the spires are long lasting in cut flower arrangements. Plants also can be left in the garden until autumn, then cut for dried arrangements. Because Astilbes are voracious feeders, soil fertility must be kept high and liberal amounts of organic matter applied to maintain vigor. Divide every 3 years.
Hardy Zones: 3-7.
Grows: 36" (90cm).
Culture: Does best in moist soil high in organic matter.
Spacing: 15-18" (38-45cm).

ASTILBE CHINENSIS 'PUMILA' ◑ ⋙
(Dwarf Chinese Astilbe)

This is a mat forming creeping perennial producing rosy pink fleecy flowers in July and August. Foliage makes a crisp green mantle above which flowers appear. Like standard varieties, Dwarf Chinese Astilbe prefers moist, organic soil and partial shade. However, it is not so moisture dependent as standard forms. The plant makes an attractive groundcover or foreground to the perennial border.
Hardy Zones: 4-8.
Grows: 12" (30cm).
Culture: Does best in moist soil high in organic matter. Needs a winter mulch of leaves, straw or hay and regular feeding program.
Spacing: 12-15" (30-38cm).

PURPLE ROCK CRESS

FALSE INDIGO

PURPLE ROCK CRESS (Detail)

BERGENIA

AUBRIETA LEICHTLINII ○ ◑ ⋙ ▲
(Purple Rock Cress)

Purple Rock Cress is a spreading perennial producing mats of evergreen foliage that are covered with small purple flowers in April and May. The strain Giant Superbissima produces bloom colors other than purple, including rose, lilac and deep red. These are excellent plants for trailing over rock walls, between boulders in the rock garden and as foreground in the flower border.
Hardy Zones: 4-9.
Grows: 4-6" (10-15cm).
Culture: Does best in well-drained soils.
Spacing: 15-18" (38-45cm).

BAPTISIA AUSTRALIS ○ ◑ ✄
(False Indigo)

Tall-growing perennial is attractive near the back of a flower border. Intense blue pea-like flowers are borne on erect stalks. Foliage is blue-green and remains handsome throughout the growing season.
Hardy Zones: 3-9.
Grows: 36-48" (90-120cm).

Culture: Does best in moist, but well-drained soil of neutral or slightly acid pH.
Spacing: 18-24" (45-60cm).

BELLIS PERENNIS ○
(English Daisy)

English Daisies are clump-growing perennials producing dark green leaves from the plant's base. Flowers appear in early spring and blooming continues until early summer. Bloom colors include shades of red, pink, blue and white in either open centered or double styles. In Zones 3-5, plants need to be dug in the fall and placed in a cold frame, then covered with a straw mulch. Even south of Zone 5, plants need to be treated as biennials; dug, separated and planted every two years to replenish plant vigor.
Hardy Zones: 6-10.
Grows: 6" (15cm).
Culture: Does best in moist soil to which heavy amounts of organic mulch has been added.
Spacing: 8-10" (20-25cm).

ENGLISH DAISY

CARPATHIAN HAREBELL

ALKANET or
SIBERIAN BUGLOSS

CUP & SAUCER
CANTERBURY-BELLS

BERGENIA CORDIFOLIA ○ ◑ ♠ ✂
(Bergenia)

Bergenia is a spreading perennial with large heart-shaped leaves and producing flowers of pink, red, purple, white or lilac. Foliage is large and heart-shaped, making the plant attractive as a groundcover. Flowers are produced on large cluster-shaped heads in April and May. In addition to being a good groundcover, the plant is attractive in a flower border or rock garden.
Hardy Zones: 4-10.
Grows: 12-15" (30-38cm).
Culture: Prefers moist soils, but will tolerate dry conditions.
Spacing: 12-15" (30-38cm).

BRUNNERA MACROPHYLLA or ANCHUSA MYOSOTIDIFLORA ○ ◑ ●
(Alkanet or Siberian Bugloss)

Compact-growing perennial producing clusters of tiny blue Forget-Me-Not flowers in May and June. Large leaves are heart-shaped. Excellent plants for the wild-garden or near the front of a flower border.
Hardy Zones: 3-9.
Grows: 12" (30cm).
Culture: Does best in a moist soil liberally supplemented with organic mulch.
Spacing: 12-15" (30-38cm).

CAMPANULA CALYCANTHEMA ○ ◑
(Cup & Saucer Canterbury-Bells)

Although Cup & Saucer is a biennial, it is a worthwhile addition to the perennial garden. Tall-growing plants produce large cup-shaped blooms in rose, white or blue during June and July. Seeds are usually planted the summer prior to flowering. Other Canterbury-Bells include those with large pendulous bell-shaped blooms and a hose-in-hose style.
Hardy Zones: 4-10.
Grows: 18-36" (45-90cm).
Culture: Does well in nearly any well-drained soil.
Spacing: 15-18" (38-45cm).

CLUSTERED BELLFLOWER

PEACH-LEAVED BELLFLOWER

CUPID'S-DART

MOUNTAIN BLUE

CAMPANULA CARPATICA ◯ ◑
(Carpathian Harebell)

This Bellflower is one of the most dependable perennials, producing flat-cupped blue or white flowers from early summer to late fall. Flowers are borne on wiry stems above neat clumps of narrow foliage. Plants are attractive in the rock garden or as border edging.
Hardy Zones: 3-10.
Grows: 6" (15cm).
Culture: Does well in nearly any well-drained garden soil.
Spacing: 12-15" (30-38cm).

CAMPANULA GLOMERATA ◯ ◑
(Clustered Bellflower)

Clustered Bellflower cultivars are known for their blue, purple, or white bell-shaped blooms. Densely produced in upward facing clusters, flowers appear in June and July. Because of their medium size, these plants are attractive near the center of a flower border.
Hardy Zones: 4-10.
Grows: 18-24" (45-60cm).
Culture: Does best in moist, but well-drained soil.

Spacing: 15-18" (38-45cm).

CAMPANULA PERSICIFOLIA ◯ ◑
(Peach-Leaved Bellflower)

This is the most reliable perennial form of bellflower, with cultivars producing sky blue, purple or white, single bell-shaped flowers on tall stems. Foliage is narrow and rich green in color. Plant near the back of the flower border.
Hardy Zones: 4-10.
Grows: 36-48" (90-120cm).
Culture: Does best in moist, but well-drained soil.
Spacing: 15-18" (38-45cm).

CATANANCHE CAERULEA ◯ ✂
(Cupid's-Dart)

Cupid's-Dart is a narrow, upright-growing perennial producing long strap-like leaves near the plant's base and wiry stems on which blue or white flowers are borne from June to early July. Flowers resemble cornflowers, but petals are serrated. Plants are attractive in the flower border and dried buds are used in floral arrangements.

GLOBE CENTAUREA

PERSIAN CORNFLOWER

JUPITER'S-BEARD or RED VALERIAN

Hardy Zones: 5-10.
Grows: 15-18" (38-45cm).
Culture: Does best in well-drained soils.
Spacing: 8-10" (20-25cm).

CENTAUREA DEALBATA, C. MACROCEPHALA and C. MONTANA ○✕
(Perennial Cornflower)

C. dealbata or Persian Cornflower is a perennial that performs well in the flower border and is a valued source of cut flowers. Plants produce fern-like foliage and during June-July, feathery petaled flowers appear in lilac and rosy shades. In contrast, *C. macrocephala,* or Globe Centaurea, produces large yellow thistle-like blooms from mid summer until fall. Stems are nearly devoid of foliage. Another form producing feathery blooms, but more than 3" (8cm) in diameter, is *C. montana,* or Mountain Blue. This flower's bloom period is from early summer to early fall. Flowers are blue with magenta centers.
Hardy Zones: 4-8.
Grows: 30-48" (75-120cm).

Culture: Does best in well-drained soil.
Spacing: 12-18" (30-45cm).

CENTRANTHUS RUBER ○◑✕
(Jupiter's-Beard or Red Valerian)

Robust perennial producing large clusters of fragrant carmine-rose flowers from early summer until late fall. Foliage is large, rich green and heart-shaped. This is a good perennial for the novice gardener because of its dependable bloom. Cutting flowers often will stimulate additional production. An attractive perennial near the back of the flower border.
Hardy Zones: 4-9.
Grows: 24-36" (60-90cm).
Culture: Does well in nearly any well-drained soil.
Spacing: 15-18" (38-45cm).

CUSHION or HARDY MUM

CUSHION or HARDY MUM

CUSHION or HARDY MUM

SHASTA DAISY DOUBLE

CERASTIUM TOMENTOSUM ○ ₩♠
(Snow-In-Summer)

Low-growing, spreading perennial producing dainty white flowers in late spring to early summer. Silver-gray foliage gives the plant an ornamental quality when not in bloom. Excellent as a low border, groundcover, or specimen planting in rock gardens.
Hardy Zones: 2-10.
Grows: 3-6" (8-15cm).
Culture: Does best in well-drained garden soil.
Spacing: 12-24" (30-60cm).

CHEIRANTHUS CHEIRI ○ ◑ ✂
(English Wallflower)

Although a perennial, English Wallflowers are best treated as biennials. Flowers are produced in clusters at the top of a single stalk, starting in late spring and continuing until mid summer. Foliage is long and narrow. Bloom colors include pink, red, maroon, brown, mahogany and purple. They are noted for their long-lasting attractiveness in bouquets.
Hardy Zones: 5-9.

Grows: 9-18" (23-45cm).
Culture: Perform best in well-drained, alkaline soils.
Spacing: 6-12" (15-30cm).

CHELONE LYONII ◑
(Pink Turtlehead)

This unusual perennial produces short spikes of pink flowers from early summer to early fall. Foliage is large and glossy green. This is a good plant for partially shaded areas that have liberal amounts of moisture.
Hardy Zones: 4-9.
Grows: 24-36" (60-90cm).
Culture: Does best in moist, organically rich soils.
Spacing: 15-18" (38-45cm).

CHRYSANTHEMUM COCCINEUM or PYRETHRUM ROSEUM ○ ◑ ✂
(Painted Daisy)

Painted Daisy is a medium-growing perennial producing large daisy-like or double blooms from early to midsummer. Bloom colors are white, pink and red. Most

PAINTED DAISY

ENGLISH WALLFLOWER

SNOW-IN-SUMMER

SHASTA DAISY SINGLE

widely grown are Robinson Hybrids, E.M. Robinson of which is illustrated above. All display fernlike foliage and make long-lasting cut flowers.

Hardy Zones: 4-10.

Grows: 18" (45cm).

Culture: Perform best in soils that have been cultivated thoroughly with liberal amounts of organic matter applied.

Spacing: 12-24" (30-60cm).

CHRYSANTHEMUM MAXIMUM ○✂
(Shasta Daisy)

Shasta Daisies are showy summer flowering perennials with large single or double white blooms borne on long erect stems clothed in deep green foliage. Excellent plants for the flower border or cutting. A number of good varieties available. Shown on pages 38 and 39 are double flowered Aglaya and single Alaska, both of medium size. A unique form is Polaris, tall growing and producing blooms up to 7" (18cm) in diameter.

Hardy Zones: 4-10.

Grows: 20-48" (50-120cm).

Culture: Does best in moist, but well-drained soils high in organic matter.

Spacing: 18-24" (45-60cm).

CHRYSANTHEMUM X MORIFOLIUM ○
(Cushion or Hardy Mum)

Cushion mums can be relied upon to give a showy burst of color in mid to late autumn when little else is in bloom. Plants are mounded and covered with large blooms of various styles, depending on varieties planted. Deep green cut foliage provides an attractive background to blooms of white, orange, pink, red, copper, lavender, and bronze.

Hardy Zones: 4-10.

Grows: 9-15" (23-38cm).

Culture: Perform best in soils that have been cultivated thoroughly with liberal amounts of organic matter applied.

Spacing: 12-15" (30-38cm).

JACKMANII CLEMATIS

HENRYI CLEMATIS

HAGLEY HYBRID CLEMATIS

ELSA SPAETH CLEMATIS

CHRYSOGONUM VIRGINIANUM ○ ◑
(Chrysogonum Golden Star)

Compact-growing perennial producing bright yellow star-shaped flowers from late spring until autumn. Foliage is bright green and shaped like arrowheads. Good rock garden plant.

Hardy Zones: 5-9.
Grows: 10-12" (25-30cm).
Culture: Does best in light, but moist, acidic soils.
Spacing: 12-15" (30-38cm).

CLEMATIS

Clematis are generally thought of as vining plants that bear large showy flowers and grow 8-10' (2.4-3m). Most of these are deciduous hybrids which bloom during summer months in a wide color range. However, there are shrubby forms that are useful in the perennial border, providing unusual flowers of white or blue on plants 24-48" (60-120cm).

CLEMATIS or VIRGIN'S BOWER ○

This is the vining form, producing large flowers of a wide color range from early to late summer. Attractive plant for use on lamp posts, trellises, walls and fences. Gaining popularity are some small flowered types and the ever-green *C. armandii*. Yet, like most evergreens, this vine is suited primarily to southern gardens.

Hardy Zones: 4-9.
Grows: 8-20 ft. (2.4-6m).
Culture: Does best in moist, but well-drained soil liberally enriched with organic mulch. Although needing full sun, roots must be shaded.
Spacing: 48" (120cm).
Large flowered popular varieties include:
    Comtesse deBouchard — Lilac pink.
    Duchess of Edinburgh — Double white.
    Elsa Spaeth — Blue.
    Ernest Markham — Petunia red.
    Hagley Hybrid — Shell pink.
    Henryi — Large white.
    Jackmanii — Deep purple.
    Nelly Moser — Light mauve with pink bars.

LILY-OF-THE-VALLEY

COMTESSE DE BOUCHARD CLEMATIS

CHRYSOGONUM GOLDEN STAR

Ramona — Clear blue.
The President — Plum-purple.
Ville de Lyon — Carmine-red.

C. HERACLEIFOLIA DAVIDIANA, C. INTEGRIFO-LIA CAERULEA and C. RECTA MANDSHURICA ○
(CLEMATIS [Shrub Forms])

With the common name Fragrant Tube Clematis, *C. heracleifolia davidiana* produces clusters of small blue flowers in late summer. It is somewhat fragrant. The Solitary Blue Clematis is *C. integrifolia caerulea.* Although the shortest of the three forms, it produces large pale blue flowers, one to a stem, from early to mid summer. Manchurian Ground Clematis, *C. recta mandshurica,* is the only white blooming type, also flowering from early to mid summer. It is taller, however, and produces attractive feathery foliage.
Hardy Zones: 4-9.
Grows: 24-48″ (60-120cm).
Culture: Does best in well-drained but moist soils that

are somewhat acidic and high in organic content.
Spacing: 18-24″ (45-60cm).

CONVALLARIA MAJALIS ◗ ● ᷻ ✄
Lily-of-the-Valley

Spreading perennial groundcover producing wiry stalks with tiny white bell-shaped flowers in late spring. Two upright growing leaves are produced by each plant during the growing season. Plants spread by underground stems. Good for shaded areas.
Hardy Zones: 2-7.
Grows: 8″ (20cm).
Culture: Does best in moist soils high in organic matter, yet tolerates dry shaded areas.
Spacing: 8-12″ (20-30cm).

DELPHINIUM or LARKSPUR

COREOPSIS GRANDIFLORA, C. LANCEOLATA and C. VERTICILLATA ○✂
(Coreopsis or Tickseed)

Coreopsis makes a dazzling show throughout the summer months with their golden yellow heads of single or semi-double petals borne profusely on wiry stems. *C. lanceolata* varieties are characterized by their ferny foliage and wild growth. Similar in height are *C. verticillata* forms with slender foliage. Flowers are distinctively star-shaped, however. *C. grandiflora* varieties have strap-shaped leaves. Unique double flowered, compact-growing varieties, such as Goldfink, have *C. grandiflora* parentage. Because of their profuse blooming habit, most of these varieties only live 2-3 years, although *C. verticillata* forms are very long-lived.
Hardy Zones: 3-10.
Grows: 10-24" (25-60cm).
Culture: Performs well in nearly any garden soil having adequate drainage.
Spacing: 12" (30cm).

CORONILLA VARIA ○◑〰
(Crown Vetch)

Rampant-growing, spreading perennial flowering pink from early summer until frost. Widely used as a groundcover on steep embankments and other areas where soil is poor. The plant, once established, is extremely reliable. Because of its rampant habit, Crown Vetch should not be planted in a confined area.
Hardy Zones: 3-10.
Grows: 18" (45cm).
Culture: Performs well in nearly any soil.
Spacing: 36" (90cm).

CROCOSMIA 'LUCIFER' ○✂
(Crocosmia)

Exotic corm-produced perennial having long sword-shaped leaves. Fiery red flowers are produced from early to late summer on slender stems rising from the plant's base. Because it is only semi-hardy, it should be treated as an annual from Zone 7 north.
Hardy Zones: 8-10.
Grows: 30" (75cm).

CROCOSMIA

COREOPSIS or TICKSEED

BLUE FOUNTAIN DELPHINIUM

CROWN VETCH

Culture: Needs a sandy soil of high fertility.
Spacing: 12-15″ (30-38cm).

DELPHINIUM CHINENSE or D. GRANDIFLORUM ○✂
(Chinese Delphinium)

Dwarf-growing, long-lasting perennial producing white or blue flowers on wiry stems. Blooming continues from early to late summer if plants are cut back regularly. Good performer for near the front of a flower border.
Hardy Zones: 3-7.
Grows: 24″ (60cm).
Culture: Does best in well-drained garden soil to which large amounts of organic matter has been added.
Spacing: 12″ (30cm).

DELPHINIUM ELATUM and related varieties ○✂
(Delphinium or Larkspur)

These stately perennials make an imposing sight in any garden or border. Long flower spikes are covered with florets of blue, lavender, purple and white. Popular tall varieties include Pacific Hybrids and Belladona series and are best used in the back of the garden. These should be staked before floral heads appear, however, to remain erect. The most popular of small varieties are Blue Fountains and Connecticut Yankees. Blue Fountains have large floral heads, but plants are compact and have sturdy stalks less prone to wind damage. A shrubby form, Connecticut Yankees, are somewhat taller. Both small series are available only in mixed colors. A separate color range is available for Pacific and Belladona series. Delphiniums are usually longer lived in northern areas of the U.S. Replanting in 2-3 years is usually necessary from Zone 4 south.
Hardy Zones: 2-7.
Grows: 24-72″ (60-180cm).
Culture: Does best in well-drained garden soil to which large amounts of organic matter has been added.
Spacing: 12-24″ (30-60cm).

ALLWOOD'S PINK

BORDER PINK

PLUMED BLEEDING HEART

DIANTHUS ALLWOODII ○✂🔺
(Allwood's Pink)

A hybrid form of *Dianthus* combining the free flowering habit of border pinks with large carnation like flowers in red, white and pink plus bicolors. Flowering lasts from late spring to early fall.
Hardy Zones: 4-7.
Grows: 12-18" (30-45cm).
Culture: Does best in average well-drained soil.
Spacing: 12-15" (30-37 cm).

DIANTHUS BARBATUS ○✂🔺
(Sweet William)

Prolific producer of large flat-headed blooms in red, white, pink, and combinations of these colors during late spring. Has clump like habit and grassy leaves. Best treated as a biennial.
Hardy Zones: 4-10.
Grows: 6-24" (15-60cm), depending on variety.
Culture: Does best where soil is well drained.
Spacing: 12" (30cm).

DIANTHUS PLUMARIUS ○✂🔺
(Border Pink)

Perennial producing double or fringed blooms in pink, rose, purple and white from mid to late spring. Foliage grows in grassy clumps.
Hardy Zones: 4-7.
Grows: 12-15" (30-38cm). New dwarf forms 5-7", (13-18cm).
Culture: Does best where soil is well drained.
Spacing: 12-15" (30-38cm) for standard varieties; 10-12" (25-30cm) for dwarfs.

DIANTHUS SPOTTI ○✂🔺
(Spotti Border Pink)

A unique dwarf form of *D. plumarius* producing rose-red flowers edged and spotted in silvery white.
Hardy Zones: 4-7.
Grows: 5" (13cm).
Culture: Does best in well-drained garden soil.
Spacing: 10-12" (25-30cm).

MAIDEN PINK   **SPOTTI BORDER PINK**

SWEET WILLIAM

COMMON BLEEDING HEART

DIANTHUS DELTOIDES ○✂▲
(Maiden Pink)

Mat-forming perennial producing rose-pink to crimson blooms in June. Foliage is grass like in appearance.
Hardy Zones: 4–7.
Grows: 6″ (15cm).
Culture: Does best in well-drained garden soil.
Spacing: 12″ (30cm).

DIANTHUS CAESIUS or ○✂▲
D. GRATIANOPOLITANUS
(Cheddar or Pincushion Pink)

Clump forming dwarf pink producing small carnation shaped blooms in late spring. Flowers range from clear pink to rose red depending on variety. Foliage is narrow and evergreen. Excellent rock garden, rock wall or border foreground plant. Best treated as a biennial.
Hardy Zones: 4-7.
Grows: 4-6″ (12-15cm).
Culture: Does best in well-drained garden soil.
Spacing: 6-8″ (15-20cm).

DICENTRA EXIMEA ○◑✂
(Plumed Bleeding Heart)

Producer of pendulous light pink flowers from late spring to late summer. Foliage fern like.
Hardy Zones: 4-10.
Grows: 18″ (45cm).
Culture: Prefers light shade and average garden soils.
Spacing: 15-18″ (38-45cm).

DICENTRA SPECTABILIS ○◑✂
(Common Bleeding Heart)

Pendulous pink heart shaped flowers are produced from mid to late spring. White form, *D.s. 'Alba',* also available. Both have attractive light green foliage.
Hardy Zones: 4-10.
Grows: 24-30″, (60-75cm).
Culture: Prefers light shade in average soil, but tolerates full sun where soil is moist.
Spacing: 24-36″ (60-90cm).

FOXGLOVE

CAUCASIAN LEOPARD'S-BANE

GAS PLANT

DICTAMNUS ALBUS GIGANTEUS and
D. A. PURPUREUS ○ ◐ ✂
(Gas Plant)

These reliable shrubby perennials are named for emissions of flammable fumes if roots are cut. Rich green, glossy foliage has a lemon fragrance and also produces an oily flammable substance if rubbed. These perennials produce tall spikes of white or purple-pink flowers in early summer. Both white and purple forms produce attractive seed pods that are used in dried arrangements.
Hardy Zones: 3-8.
Grows: 30-36" (75-90cm).
Culture: Does well in moist, but well-drained soils enriched with compost.
Spacing: 36" (90cm).

DIGITALIS PURPUREA HYBRIDS ○ ◐ ✂
(Foxglove)

These are striking tall-growing biennials for the back of the flower border, producing tubular blooms in a wide color range. Popular mixed strains include Excelsior, Foxy and Giant Shirley. Good perennial forms include

the dwarf *D. ambigua,* producing yellow flowers marked with brown and growing to just 24" (60cm). Somewhat taller, producing strawberry-pink flowers, is *D. mertonensis,* blooming from June through August.
Hardy Zones: 4-10.
Grows: 24-48", (60-120cm).
Culture: Does best in moist, but well-drained garden soils.
Spacing: 12-15" (30-38cm).

DORONICUM CAUCASICUM ○ ◐ ✂
(Caucasian Leopard's-Bane)

Although there are perennial Leopard's-Banes that grow nearly 60" (150cm), the most popular forms belong to the *D. caucasicum* group, which grow 18-24" (45-60cm). All produce showy, daisy-like golden blooms in April and May. Heart-shaped foliage is produced near the base of each plant. These are good border perennials and attractive cut flowers.
Hardy Zones: 4-9.
Grows: 18-24" (45-60cm).
Culture: Does best in moist, but well-drained soil.
Spacing: 12" (30cm).

MOCK STRAWBERRY

YELLOW FLEABANE

GLOBE HYBRIDS

LAVENDER FLEABANE

DUCHESNEA INDICA ○ ◑ ⋈
(Mock Strawberry)

Striking groundcover with strawberrylike foliage, spreading by runners which form a mat 2-3" (5-8cm) deep. Small flowers resemble those of large strawberry varieties, but are yellow instead of white. Small red bitter berries are produced above the foliage in mid summer. Foliage retains its green color into autumn.
Hardy Zones: 2-10.
Grows: 4" (10cm).
Culture: Does well in nearly any soil.
Spacing: 12-18" (30-45cm).

ECHINOPS HYBRIDS ○ ✂
(Globe Hybrids)

Two varieties of this unusual perennial are on the market today. Both feature globe-shaped thistle heads, produced in July, and large, coarse, deeply cut foliage. Ritro, however, has metallic blue flowers, while Taplow Blue produces blooms that are violet-blue with silver tips. Both make good accent plants in the border and floral heads are attractive in dried arrangements.

Hardy Zones: 3-10.
Grows: 30-36" (75-90cm).
Culture: Does best in well-drained soil and tolerates droughty conditions.
Spacing: 18-24" (45-60cm).

EPIMEDIUM GRANDIFLORUM and *E. YOUNGIANUM 'NIVEUM'* ◑ ● ⋈
(Barrenwort)

Epimediums are compact-growing, spreading plants featuring heart-shaped leaves. In early spring the various cultivars produce white, red, yellow or pink star-shaped flowers in abundance. Plants spread through their root systems. Good edging plants.
Hardy Zones: 3-8.
Grows: 8-12" (20-30cm).
Culture: Does well in nearly any soil that retains moisture.
Spacing: 8-10" (20-25cm).

HARDY AGERATUM or MIST FLOWER

MYRTLE EUPHORBIA

CUSHION SPURGE

PURPLELEAF WINTERCREEPER

ERIGERON HYBRIDS ○ ✂
(Fleabane)

These are reliable perennials that are attractive in the flower border. Blue or violet-blue flowers, either single or semi-double have bright yellow centers. Blooms are produced from June through September above narrow foliage. Unusual to the group is the deep pink semi hybrid Foerster's Darling. The Fleabanes also include a golden headed, but rather short lived perennial named *E. aurantiacus.* Because of its compact habit, it is useful near the front of a flower border or in containers. The true perennial Fleabanes are ideal for cutting.
Hardy Zones: 4-10.
Grows: 18-24" (45-60cm).
Culture: Does best in well-drained, sandy soils.
Spacing: 12" (30cm).

ERYNGIUM AMETHYSTINUM ○ ✂
(Amethyst Sea Holly)

Unusual perennial producing blue spiky flowers from mid summer until autumn. Plant is bushy and foliage is narrow and spiked. Good for dry sandy areas where little else

will grow. Dried flowers are attractive in floral arrangements.
Hardy Zones: 4-10.
Grows: 24" (60cm).
Culture: Does best in sandy, infertile, well-drained soils.
Spacing: 12-18" (30-45cm).

EUONYMUS FORTUNEI 'COLORATUS' ○ ◑ ●
(Purpleleaf Wintercreeper)   〰➤ ▲

Hardy, dense-growing groundcover of spreading habit. Green foliage turns bronze in late fall. Because of its rooting habit, it makes an excellent groundcover for embankments.
Hardy Zones: 4-10.
Grows: 12-15" (30-38cm).
Culture: Does best in soils heavily enriched with organic mulch.
Spacing: 12-24" (30-60cm).

EUPATORIUM COELESTINUM ○ ◑ ✂
(Hardy Ageratum or Mist Flower)

Valuable to the fall flower border because of late summer

AMETHYST SEA HOLLY

BARRENWORT

MEADOWSWEET

SUN GOD BLANKET FLOWER

blooming habit. Clusters of purple-blue flowers are produced from August until frost on purple stems. Foliage is coarse and toothy.
Hardy Zones: 4-10.
Grows: 18-36" (45-90cm).
Culture: Does well in nearly any well-drained soil.
Spacing: 18-24" (45-60cm).

EUPHORBIA EPITHYMOIDES or *E. POLYCHROMA* ○
(Cushion Spurge)

Mound-shaped Spurge that gradually spreads to 24" (60cm). In late spring the plant is covered with bright yellow bracts. Foliage turns red in autumn.
Hardy Zones: 4-9.
Grows: 12" (30cm).
Culture: Does best in well-drained soil.
Spacing: 18-24" (45-60cm).

EUPHORBIA MYRSINITES ○ ⋙
(Myrtle Euphorbia)

Attractive perennial with trailing habit producing thick

blue-green leaves. Although green flowers are produced in late spring, most noticeable are yellow bracts. Good rockgarden plant.
Hardy Zones: 4-9.
Grows: 6" (15cm).
Culture: Does best in well-drained soil.
Spacing: 18-24" (45-60cm).

FILIPENDULA HEXAPETALA or *F. VULGARIS* ◑
(Meadowsweet)

Showy, easily grown perennial producing white flowers from June to August. Single and double flowered varieties are available. Foliage is fernlike.
Hardy Zones: 4-8.
Grows: 15-18" (38-45cm).
Culture: Does best in moist soils, but tolerates dry conditons.
Spacing: 12" (30cm).

RED CRANESBILL GERANIUM

DAZZLER BLANKET FLOWER

GENTIAN

GAILLARDIA ARISTATA ○✂
(Blanket Flower or Fiesta Daisy)

Blanket Flowers are showy perennials that bloom over a long period from early summer to frost. Slender stems carry daisy-type blooms in gold, gold and red and maroon, depending on variety. Foliage is narrow and hairy. Growth ranges from under 12" (30cm) to 24" (60cm) or more. Dazzler, illustrated above, is of medium size, featuring golden yellow flowers with maroon centers. Goblin or Baby Cole are popular dwarfs, while Burgundy and Sun God are tall. Burgundy has red flowers, while Sun God is yellow.
Hardy Zones: 3-10.
Grows: 8-24" (20-60cm).
Culture: Does best on well-drained soils and known for drought resistance.
Spacing: 10-12" (25-30cm).

GENTIANA ACAULIS and G. SEPTEMFIDA ◐ ●
(Gentian)

Gentians are popular flowers for rock garden plantings because of their compact growth habit. Trumpet-shaped flowers appear on *G. acaulis* in spring months. *G. septemfida* flowers in late summer. While both types have blue flowers, *G. acaulis* blooms are brighter blue and petals curl back. *G. septemfida* flowers are more scalloped. Although both like a partially shaded location, *G. acaulis* tolerates a more exposed site.
Hardy Zones: 4-8.
Grows: 4-8" (10-20cm).
Culture: Grow in acidic soils rich in organic matter.
Spacing: 10-15" (25-38cm).

GERANIUM ENDRESSII, G. GRANDIFLORUM, G. SANGUINEUM and hybrids ○ ◐
(Cranesbill Geranium)

Cranesbill Geraniums are characterized by spreading habit and profuse blooms in magenta, white, shades of blue and lavender. Densely branched plants are heavily clothed in deeply cut foliage bright to gray-green in color. All bloom over a long period, providing garden color from early to late summer. Russell Prichard is a popular variety with magenta cup-shaped blooms and mounded habit. It is also one of the dwarf varieties, attaining only 6"

BORIS' AVENS

BLUE CRANESBILL GERANIUM

MRS. STRATHEDEN AVENS

RUSSELL PRICHARD CRANESBILL GERANIUM

(15cm) in height. *Geranium grandiflorum* is blue flowering and has a similar spreading habit as other more vigorous varieties. *G. sanguineum,* while a brighter red than Russell Prichard, is more robust. Flowers appear similar to annual Impatiens in shape and foliage is more lacy than other cranesbills, turning blood-red in fall. The most vigorous of the group is Wargrave Pink, a hybrid of *G. endressii.* This variety produces clear pink flowers and attains a height of 18″ (45cm). All of the Cranesbill Geraniums are relatively easy to grow, doing well with little maintenance. However, *G. sanguineum* varieties will need to be divided after 3-4 seasons to renew vigor.

Hardy Zones: 4-8.
Grows: 6-18″ (15-45cm).
Culture: Does well in nearly any garden soil.
Spacing: 12-15″ (30-38cm).

GEUM 'BORISII' and GEUM CHILOENSE ○
(Geum or Avens)

Geum or Avens are colorful perennials blooming during summer months in yellow, red and orange shades. Although flowers are borne wildly on tall wiry stems, plants are not invasive. *G. chiloense* foliage is deeply cut, while that of *G. 'borisii'* is more fan-shaped and produced closer to the plant's base. Although flowers are produced from early summer until August, the bloom period can be extended into autumn by trimming spent floral heads. *G. 'borisii'* is a brilliant orange semi-double. Many varieties are produced from *Geum chiloense,* including the popular double yellow Mrs. Stratheden and scarlet double Mrs. Bradshaw.

Hardy Zones: 5-10.
Grows: 18-24″ (45-60cm).
Culture: Grow in moist, but well-drained soils high in organic matter.
Spacing: 10-12″ (25-30cm).

BABY'S BREATH

CREEPING BABY'S BREATH

ENGLISH IVY

HELEN'S FLOWER

GYPSOPHILA PANICULATA ○✂
(Baby's Breath)

Airy, graceful perennial producing thousands of small white flowers in early summer. Bristol Fairy, the most common hybrid, grows 36" (90cm) tall and equally wide. A smaller variety, Pink Fairy produces masses of double light pink blooms. Excellent as cut flowers.

Hardy Zones: 4-8.
Grows: 36" (90cm).
Culture: Best in well-drained, somewhat alkaline soils.
Spacing: 18-24" (45-60cm).

GYPSOPHILA REPENS ○ ⋙
(Creeping Baby's Breath)

This trailing perennial produces white or pink flowers April through May. Blooms are star-shaped with deep rose centers. Excellent plant for embankments and rock gardens and walls.

Hardy Zones: 4-8.
Grows: 6" (15cm).
Culture: Best in well-drained, somewhat alkaline soils.
Spacing: 18-24" (45-60cm).

HEDERA HELIX ● ⋙▲✂
(English Ivy)

This popular groundcover forms a lush carpet in partially sunny or shady areas. Woody stems, which root as they grow, control soil erosion. Many varieties are available. Algerian Ivy, *Hedera canariensis,* a more robust plant fills barren areas even more quickly. Leaves are three-lobed and nearly twice the size of English Ivy but its use is more limited because of a Zone 7 hardiness. It also roots as it spreads.

Hardy Zones: 5-10.
Grows: 6-12" (15-30cm).
Culture: Needs a moist soil high in organic matter.
Spacing: 12" (30cm). Algerian Ivy: 18" (45cm).

HELENIUM AUTUMNALE ○✂
(Helen's Flower)

Autumn blooming, *Helenium* produces masses of golden to mahogany-red daisylike blooms from late July until frost. Flowers produced on top of long stems. Attractive in the flower border. Excellent cut flowers.

Hardy Zones: 3-10.

PERENNIAL SUNFLOWER

SUN ROSE

FALSE SUNFLOWER or ROUGH HELIOPSIS

Grows: 36-48" (90-120cm).
Culture: Does well in nearly any garden soil, but growth is better where soil is moist.
Spacing: 12-18" (30-45cm).

HELIANTHEMUM MUTABILE or H. NUMMULARIFOLIUM ○ ᴡᴡ▲
(Sun Rose)

A compact-growing perennial or subshrub producing evergreen foliage on woody stems with a trailing habit. Yellow, white, pink, apricot or red flowers from mid to late summer. Ideal for groundcover, rock garden or as a foreground to flower border.
Hardy Zones: 4-10.
Grows: 6-10" (15-25cm).
Culture: Does well in nearly any garden soil.
Spacing: 18" (45cm).

HELIANTHUS DECAPETALUS FLORE PLENO ○
(Perennial Sunflower)

These are large perennials for growing near the back of the flower border, producing golden yellow dahlia-like blooms from mid to late summer. Foliage is large and coarse.
Hardy Zones: 3-10.
Grows: 48" (120cm).
Culture: Does well in nearly any garden soil.
Spacing: 18-24" (45-60cm).

HELIOPSIS SCABRA ○✂
(False Sunflower or Rough Heliopsis)

Showy perennial producing large golden yellow blooms from July until frost. Flower heads are large, nearly double and produced on erect stalks clothed with dark green leaves. Attractive in the flower border and excellent cut flowers.
Hardy Zones: 3-9.
Grows: 30" (75cm).
Culture: Does best in moist soil rich in organic matter.
Spacing: 24" (60cm).

CORAL BELLS

RUPTUREWORT

CHRISTMAS ROSE

HELLEBORUS NIGER ◑ ✄
(Christmas Rose)

Depending on climate, Christmas Rose produces large white flowers with yellow or rosy centers, from late autumn until spring. Foliage is narrow, leatherlike and evergreen. Plants are bushy. Related is Lenten Rose, *Helleborus orientalis,* producing white, purple, brown or greenish flowers from early to mid spring. It also has leathery evergreen foliage. Christmas and Lenten roses make good cut flowers if stems are seared with a match before placing in water.

Hardy Zones: 4-8.
Grows: 12-15″ (30-38cm).
Culture: Does best in moist, somewhat alkaline soil enriched with organic mulch.
Spacing: 12-15″ (30-38cm).

HEMEROCALLIS HYBRIDS ○ ◑ ✄
(Daylily)

The Daylily is a reliable perennial producing long rush-like leaves and showy large flowers with interesting stamens in a multitude of colors. Depending on variety, bloom time ranges from early spring until frost. Recent hybridization has also affected height, so that it is now possible to buy varieties from 1½-4′ (45-120cm) tall. Although blooms do not last very long, the profuse blooming habit and length of season compensates. Spent blooms should be picked regularly to encourage further flowering. Although most daylilies die back in winter months, a number remain evergreen and need winter application of straw from Zone 5 north. Daylilies are good flowers for the perennial border. Blooms are colorful in cut bouquets, but short-lived.

Hardy Zones: 4-10.
Grows: 18-48″ (45-120cm).
Culture: Does best in moist, but well-drained soils high in organic matter.
Spacing: 18-24″ (45-60cm).

HERNIARIA GLABRA ○ ⌇⌇
(Rupturewort)

This trailing perennial produces a dense mat of low-growing, moss-like foliage, which is ideal for groundcover, rock gardens or walkway edgings. Giving orna-

54

COPPER DAYLILY

CORAL DAYLILY

YELLOW DAYLILY

mental value is their production of small green flowers from July until late August.

Hardy Zones: 5-9.
Grows: 2″ (5cm).
Culture: Does well in a variety of locations, even where soil is poor.
Spacing: 10-12″ (25-30cm).

HESPERIS MATRONALIS ○ ◑
(Dame's Rocket or Sweet Rocket)

Dame's Rocket is an easy to grow perennial that has become wild in many parts of the U.S. and Europe. Plants are upright, producing loose Phlox like floral heads of purple, lilac or white from May to mid July. If spent blooms are removed, flowering can be extended into early autumn. Although relatively short lived, the plant comes easily from seed. Sowing some seed each year is recommended for having a good stand of flowering plants the following spring.

Hardy Zones: 4-8.
Grows: 24-36″ (60-90cm).
Culture: Does best in moist, but well-drained soil.

Spacing: 15-18″ (38-45cm).

HEUCHERA SANGUINEA ○ ◑ ✄
(Coral Bells)

Coral Bells is a reliable perennial producing metallic-green heart-shaped leaves, mounded in habit. Tall wiry stems bear small bell-shaped flowers from late spring to July in colors ranging from ivory-white to deep rose-red. As a series, Bressingham hybrids produce the most complete color range. Plants expand through their long fleshy roots. Divide every 5-6 years to avoid overcrowding. Mulch with straw or evergreen boughs in late Fall to avoid winter heave.

Hardy Zones: 4-10.
Grows: 24″ (60cm).
Culture: Does best in moist, but well-drained soil high in organic matter.
Spacing: 12″ (30cm).

HOSTA 'ROYAL STANDARD'

HOSTA 'FRANCEE'

HOSTA UNDULATA 'VARIEGATA'

HOSTA VARIETIES ○ ◑ ●
(Plantain Lily)

Plantain Lilies or Hostas continue to grow in popularity as gardeners discover their beauty and function around their homes. Plants are mound-shaped and feature large attractive leaves from deep blue to light green. A wide range of variegated leaf forms have come onto the market in recent years. Providing contrast to the rather somber green and blue-green leaf colors are gold, ivory and silvery white variegation. Each kind produces tall bell-shaped flowers during mid summer. Bloom colors include white, pink, blue and lavender. Hostas perform best where there is a moist soil rich in organic matter. However, they are noted for their tolerance of dry shady areas. Because of this trait, Hostas are widely used at the base of trees and near shrubs. They also make good low hedges for lining paved areas. Some of the larger varieties are attractive accents in a flower border. When mass planted, Hostas make good groundcover in no traffic areas. They are among the most reliable perennials, performing well year after year with a minimum of care. Some of the more attractive forms appear on these pages and are described in some detail below:

Hardy Zones: 3-9
Grow: 12-30″ (30-75cm)
Culture: Do well in nearly any garden soil. Tolerate dry conditions.
Spacing: 18-24″ (45-60cm).

Hosta 'August Moon'—Robust-growing variety producing large rounded golden yellow foliage. White flowers appear on 36″ (90cm) stems in mid summer.

Hosta 'Gold Standard'—Outstanding variety with light green leaves in spring turning gold with light green margins by summer. Morning sunshine is recommended to bring out gold color.

Hosta fortunei 'Aureo-Marginata'—One of the most widely grown varieties with dark green leaves outlined in gold. Lilac colored blooms appear on 24″ (60cm) stems in mid summer.

Hosta fortunei 'Hyacinthina'—Attractive variety producing large mound of green to blue-gray foliage. Pale lav-

HOSTA 'AUGUST MOON'

HOSTA UNDULATA 'ALBO-MARGINATA'

HOSTA FORTUNEI 'HYACINTHINA'

HOSTA FORTUNEI 'AUREO-MARGINATA'

HOSTA SIEBOLDIANA 'ELEGANS'

ender flowers are produced on 24″ (60cm) stems in mid summer.

Hosta 'Francee' — Compact-growing variety featuring rich green foliage with distinctive white edges. Soft lavender-blue flowers are produced during mid summer.

Hosta 'Frances Williams' — Handsome *sieboldiana* type. Blue-green foliage has wide golden yellow borders. White flowers are produced on 18″ (45cm) stems.

Hosta plantaginea — This is an old fashioned Hosta species commonly known as Fragrant Hosta. White flowers are produced in late summer. Foliage is large, heart shaped and light green, forming a mound up to 3′ (90cm) in diameter.

Hosta 'Royal Standard' — Large variety with rich green foliage. Fragrant white flowers are produced on 36″ (90cm) stems during mid summer. One of few varieties that performs well in full sun.

Hosta sieboldiana 'Elegans' — One of the largest growing

varieties featuring blue-green foliage and white flowers that appear on 40″ (100cm) stems during July.

Hosta undulata 'Albo-Marginata' — Handsome mounded plants have large deep green leaves with white margins. Lavender blooms appear in August on 24″ (60cm) stems.

Hosta undulata 'Erromena' — Produces large wavy leaves of dark green. Light violet flowers appear in August on 24″ (60cm) stems.

Hosta undulata 'Variegata' — A most attractive variety featuring white and green wavy leaves. Lilac blooms on 36″ (90cm) stems appear in July.

These are just a few of the many varieties available. Check with your local nurseryman or grower for his recommendations.

ST. JOHN'S-WORT

HARDY GLOXINIA

CANDYTUFT

SUNRAY FLOWER

HYPERICUM CALYCINUM ○ ⚬
(St. John's-Wort)

St. John's-Wort is a spreading perennial with woody stems and bright yellow summer flowers. Underground rooting system binds the soil, making the plant a good hillside groundcover. Foliage is evergreen in warm climates.
Hardy Zones: 6-10.
Grows: 12" (30cm).
Culture: Does well in nearly any garden soil.
Spacing: 15-24" (38-60cm).

IBERIS SEMPERVIRENS ○ ⚬▲
(Candytuft)

Compact growing perennial producing flat clusters of white flowers in late spring. Foliage is narrow and evergreen. Spreading habit makes the plant useful in the rock garden or as edging.
Hardy Zones: 3-10.
Grows: 12" (30cm).
Culture: Does best in well-drained soil.
Spacing: 12-15" (30-38cm).

INCARVILLEA DELAVAYI ○ ◑
(Hardy Gloxinia)

A somewhat tender perennial reserved for Zone 5 and south. Large pink to rose-purple tube-shaped flowers are produced on narrow stems above serrated foliage from mid spring to mid summer.
Hardy Zones: 5-10.
Grows: 12-18" (30-45cm).
Culture: Does well in organically rich soils.
Spacing: 12-15" (30-38cm).

INULA ENSIFOLIA ○✂
(Sunray Flower)

Inulas are large golden flowers with fine rays. Golden Beauty is a popular variety of shrubby habit and long flowering period. Division may be necessary after 2 years because of overcrowding.
Hardy Zones: 3-9.
Grows: 16-24" (40-60cm).
Culture: Does well in nearly any garden soil.
Spacing: 12-18" (30-45cm).

BEARDED IRIS

SIBERIAN IRIS

JAPANESE IRIS

DWARF IRIS

IRIS X GERMANICA ○✕
(Bearded Iris)

Bearded Iris, with their large floral heads produced in a vast range of colors, continues to be a popular May flowering perennial. Blue-green foliage is straplike and plants do well season after season with only minimal care.
Hardy Zones: 3-10.
Grows: 30-35" (75-88cm).
Culture: Does best in well-drained soil.
Spacing: 10-15" (25-38cm).

IRIS KAEMPFERI ○✕
(Japanese Iris)

Exotic tall perennial with erect sword-shaped foliage. Flowers are produced from early to mid summer. Blooms are flat, and are produced in white, purple, blue and violet, depending on variety. Good for planting near a pond.
Hardy Zones: 5-8.
Grows: 36" (90cm).
Culture: Needs moist soil high in organic matter and low in pH.

Spacing: 15-18" (38-45cm).

IRIS PUMILA ○
(Dwarf Iris)

Dwarf versions of Bearded Iris, these also come in a wide color range, although most popular colors are yellow-gold, purple, blue, burgundy, white and two-toned. Bloom period is from mid spring to early summer.
Hardy Zones: 3-10.
Grows: 6-8" (15-20cm).
Culture: Does best in well-drained soil.
Spacing: 10-12" (25-30cm).

IRIS SIBIRICA ○✕
(Siberian Iris)

Although Siberian Iris appear similar to Bearded Iris, petals are narrower and do not have a beard. They produce flowers of violet, purple, white or blue in mid summer.
Hardy Zones: 3-8.
Grows: 36" (90cm).
Culture: Does best in moist, but well-drained soil.
Spacing: 15-18" (38-45cm).

RED HOT POKER

DEAD NETTLE

PERENNIAL PEA

PFITZER RED HOT POKER

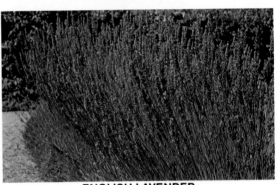

ENGLISH LAVENDER

KNIPHOFIA UVARIA HYBRIDS ○✂
(Tritoma or Red Hot Poker)

Tritoma is an attractive perennial producing long poker shaped flower heads of orange, yellow or red from early August to mid October. Foliage is long and grasslike. Springtime, an orange and ivory bicolor; and Primrose Beauty, pastel yellow, are tall varieties. *K. pfitzeri* is a solid orange variety and more compact in habit at 24" (60cm).
Hardy Zones: 5-10.
Grows: 24-30" (60-75cm).
Culture: Does best in well-drained soil. Should have winter protection of straw or other mulch.
Spacing: 18-24" (45-60cm).

LAMIUM GALEOBDOLON
and *L. MACULATUM* ○◑●↝
(Dead Nettle)

Dead Nettles are quick spreading groundcovers that do well in shaded, dry areas. *L. galeobdolon* varieties spread by runners and produce yellow flowers in May. Foliage is green and silver. *L. maculatum* varieties include

Chequers and Beacon Silver. Both produce pink flowers above variegated foliage starting in April. Chequers has bright green foliage with creamy midribs, while Beacon Silver produces silvery green heart-shaped leaves with deep green margins. Beacon Silver also is more compact growing and less invasive to neighboring plants.
Hardy Zones: 3-9.
Grows: 4-8" (10-20cm).
Culture: Does well in nearly any garden soil.
Spacing: 12-15" (30-38cm).

LATHYRUS LATIFOLIUS ○◑↝✂
(Perennial Pea)

This vining perennial produces clusters of Sweet Pea blooms in pink, red, purple and white from early summer until fall. Plants are good climbers attractive on trellises, fences or boulders.
Hardy Zones: 3-10.
Grows: 4-8' (1.2-2.4m).
Culture: Does best in well-drained garden soil.
Spacing: 24" (60cm).

EDELWEISS

PERENNIAL FLAX

DWARF GOLDEN FLAX

SPIKE GAYFEATHER

LAVANDULA ANGUSTIFOLIA and *HYBRIDS* ○▲
(English Lavender)

English Lavender has aromatic gray-green foliage and scented flower spikes. Flowers are deep purple, lavender or pink, depending on variety. The plant is attractive in the flower border, rock garden and along a garden path. Major hybrids include Hidcote, deep purple; Munstead, lavender; and Jean Davis, off white or light pink.
Hardy Zones: 5-10.
Grows: 12-18″ (30-45cm).
Culture: Does best in well-drained soil.
Spacing: 15-18″ (38-45cm).

LEONTOPODIUM ALPINUM ○ ⋎⋎
(Edelweiss)

This alpine wildflower, now in wide cultivation, is an eye-catching rock plant. Foliage is woolly white and flowers are really floral leaves set in star-shaped clusters, which appear in June and July.
Hardy Zones: 5-8.
Grows: 6″ (15cm).

Culture: Does best in well-drained soil.
Spacing: 8-10″ (20-25cm).

LIATRIS PYCNOSTACHYA and *L. SPICATA* ○◑✂
(Kansas Gayfeather and Spike Gayfeather)

Gayfeathers are unique, producing tall spikes of feathery flowers, which open from the top of each stalk downward. Kansas Gayfeather is tallest, producing lavender-pink or white flowers in late summer. At half the height of Kansas, Kobold Spike Gayfeather produces rose-lavender flowers from July to September. Both are good border plants.
Hardy Zones: 3-10.
Grows: 24-72″ (60-180cm).
Culture: Does best in well-drained soil.
Spacing: 12-15″ (30-38cm).

CARDINAL FLOWER

LUPINE or BLUE BONNET

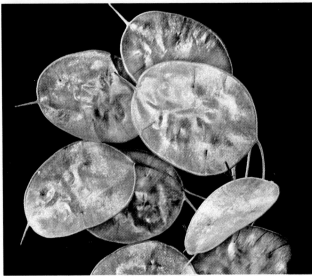

MONEY PLANT

MALTESE-CROSS

LINUM PERENNE ○
(Perennial Flax)

L. perenne is a reliable perennial producing dainty blue or white blooms on slender stems from early summer until late fall. Foliage is rich green and feathery. Another blue flowered form is *L. narbonense,* although blooms have white centers. Blooming period is from mid spring to early summer. A yellow form is *L. flavum,* with the dwarf *L. flavum 'Compactum'* most attractive. These perennials produce rich green foliage and transparent bright yellow flowers in June and July.

Hardy Zones: 5-10.
Grows: 10-18" (25-45cm).
Culture: Does best in well-drained soil.
Spacing: 15-18" (38-45cm).

LOBELIA CARDINALIS ○ ◑
(Cardinal Flower)

Robust-growing perennial producing large spikes of fiery red blooms from July until October. Large green foliage is produced near plant base. *Lobelia alba* is similar in habit, but produces large white blooms and is somewhat

more compact at 30" (75cm). Both are excellent plants for damp soils.

Hardy Zones: 4-9.
Grows: 36-48" (90-120cm).
Culture: Does best in moist soils.
Spacing: 18-24" (45-60cm).

LUNARIA BIENNIS or L. ANNUA ○ ◑ ✂
(Money Plant)

Attractive shrubby plant grown for its silvery white seed-pods. Although a biennial, it is an attractive accent in the perennial border. Sweet scented blue, pink or white flowers are produced in late spring to early summer. Seed pods are widely used in dried bouquets.

Hardy Zones: 5-10.
Grows: 36" (90cm).
Culture: Does well in nearly any well-drained soil.
Spacing: 12-15" (30-38cm).

LUPINUS HYBRIDS ○ ◑ ✂
(Lupine or Bluebonnet)

Lupines are some of the showiest perennials for the

GERMAN CATCHFLY

flower border, producing long spikes of brilliant colored flowers from mid spring to mid summer. Plants also produce attractive fan-shaped foliage. Bloom colors include blue, yellow, white, rose, red, and pink. Russell Hybrid is the most popular series, producing a wide color range. Attractive mass planted near the back of a flower border.
Hardy Zones: 4-7.
Grows: 3-5' (.9-1.5m).
Culture: Does best in cool, moist but well-drained soil of neutral or slightly acidic pH.
Spacing: 18" (45cm).

LYCHNIS CHALCEDONICA ○✂
(Maltese-Cross)

A summer flowering perennial bearing large scarlet globe-shaped heads of small Maltese Cross-shaped flowers. Foliage and stems are hairy and foliage is silvery green. Attractive plant for the flower border.
Hardy Zones: 3-10.
Grows: 24-36" (60-90cm).
Culture: Does well in well-drained garden soil.
Spacing: 12-15" (30-38cm).

LYCHNIS VISCARIA ○ ◑
(German Catchfly)

Catchfly is a summer blooming perennial producing rosy pink double or single flowers during June and July on wiry foliage-free stems. *L. viscaria 'Flore Plena'* is a double flowered form growing 18" (45cm) widely used for cut flowers. The single rose flowered Catchfly grows to about half this height and is a mat former. A white form of similar habit is *L. viscaria 'Alba'*. All Catchflys have rich green grasslike foliage produced at the plant base. The tall double pink variety makes a good border plant, while dwarf forms are attractive in rock gardens.
Hardy Zones: 3-10.
Grows: 10-18" (25-45cm).
Culture: Does best in well-drained garden soils.
Spacing: 12-15" (30-38cm).

PURPLE LOOSESTRIFE

CIRCLE FLOWER

CREEPING JENNY

LYSIMACHIA CLETHROIDES ○ ◑ ✕
(Loosestrife)

Tall-growing perennial producing long slender flower spikes of white flowers from August to September. This is a dense-growing mat former that produces large arrow-head-shaped, glossy green foliage.
Hardy Zones: 2-10.
Grows: 36" (90cm).
Culture: Does best in moist soil.
Spacing: 18-24" (45-60cm).

LYSIMACHIA NUMMULARIA 'AUREA' ○ ◑ ⋎⋎
(Creeping Jenny)

Low-growing, trailing perennial producing bright yellow flowers in June and July. Foliage is a bright green and penny-shaped. Rooting runners form a mat, which is useful for preventing soil erosion.
Hardy Zones: 2-10.
Grows: 2" (5cm).
Culture: Does well in nearly any moist soil.
Spacing: 12-18" (30-45cm).

LYSIMACHIA PUNCTATA ○ ◑ ✕
(Circle Flower)

Circle Flower is a medium size plant producing lemon-yellow flowers in June and July. Flowers have a light brown circle in the throat. This is the most vigorous growing of Lysimachias, spreading rapidly by underground stems.
Hardy Zones: 5-10.
Grows: 12-18" (30-45cm).
Culture: Does best in moist soil.
Spacing: 12-15" (30-38cm).

LYTHRUM SALICARIA ○ ◑
(Purple Loosestrife)

Loosestrife is an upright-growing perennial producing spikes of star-shaped flowers during June through September. Foliage is narrow, and willowlike in appearance. The Morden series is by far most popular, producing rose or pink blooms. Dropmore Purple is a rich purple of about the same height, while Firecandle, a rose-red, is somewhat less vigorous.
Hardy Zones: 3-10.

GERMAN CATCHFLY

flower border, producing long spikes of brilliant colored flowers from mid spring to mid summer. Plants also produce attractive fan-shaped foliage. Bloom colors include blue, yellow, white, rose, red, and pink. Russell Hybrid is the most popular series, producing a wide color range. Attractive mass planted near the back of a flower border.
Hardy Zones: 4-7.
Grows: 3-5' (.9-1.5m).
Culture: Does best in cool, moist but well-drained soil of neutral or slightly acidic pH.
Spacing: 18" (45cm).

LYCHNIS CHALCEDONICA ○✂
(Maltese-Cross)

A summer flowering perennial bearing large scarlet globe-shaped heads of small Maltese Cross-shaped flowers. Foliage and stems are hairy and foliage is silvery green. Attractive plant for the flower border.
Hardy Zones: 3-10.
Grows: 24-36" (60-90cm).
Culture: Does well in well-drained garden soil.
Spacing: 12-15" (30-38cm).

LYCHNIS VISCARIA ○ ◑
(German Catchfly)

Catchfly is a summer blooming perennial producing rosy pink double or single flowers during June and July on wiry foliage-free stems. *L. viscaria 'Flore Plena'* is a double flowered form growing 18" (45cm) widely used for cut flowers. The single rose flowered Catchfly grows to about half this height and is a mat former. A white form of similar habit is *L. viscaria 'Alba'*. All Catchflys have rich green grasslike foliage produced at the plant base. The tall double pink variety makes a good border plant, while dwarf forms are attractive in rock gardens.
Hardy Zones: 3-10.
Grows: 10-18" (25-45cm).
Culture: Does best in well-drained garden soils.
Spacing: 12-15" (30-38cm).

CIRCLE FLOWER

PURPLE LOOSESTRIFE

CREEPING JENNY

LYSIMACHIA CLETHROIDES ○ ◐ ✕
(Loosestrife)

Tall-growing perennial producing long slender flower spikes of white flowers from August to September. This is a dense-growing mat former that produces large arrowhead-shaped, glossy green foliage.
Hardy Zones: 2-10.
Grows: 36" (90cm).
Culture: Does best in moist soil.
Spacing: 18-24" (45-60cm).

LYSIMACHIA NUMMULARIA 'AUREA' ○ ◐ ⌇
(Creeping Jenny)

Low-growing, trailing perennial producing bright yellow flowers in June and July. Foliage is a bright green and penny-shaped. Rooting runners form a mat, which is useful for preventing soil erosion.
Hardy Zones: 2-10.
Grows: 2" (5cm).
Culture: Does well in nearly any moist soil.
Spacing: 12-18" (30-45cm).

LYSIMACHIA PUNCTATA ○ ◐ ✕
(Circle Flower)

Circle Flower is a medium size plant producing lemon-yellow flowers in June and July. Flowers have a light brown circle in the throat. This is the most vigorous growing of Lysimachias, spreading rapidly by underground stems.
Hardy Zones: 5-10.
Grows: 12-18" (30-45cm).
Culture: Does best in moist soil.
Spacing: 12-15" (30-38cm).

LYTHRUM SALICARIA ○ ◐
(Purple Loosestrife)

Loosestrife is an upright-growing perennial producing spikes of star-shaped flowers during June through September. Foliage is narrow, and willowlike in appearance. The Morden series is by far most popular, producing rose or pink blooms. Dropmore Purple is a rich purple of about the same height, while Firecandle, a rose-red, is somewhat less vigorous.
Hardy Zones: 3-10.

MONARDA or BEE BALM

VIRGINIA BLUEBELLS

FEVERFEW

Grows: 2-4' (60-120cm).
Culture: Does best in moist soil.
Spacing: 15-18" (38-45cm).

MATRICARIA CAPENSIS or *CHRYSANTHEMUM PARTHENIUM* ○✄ (Feverfew)

Feverfew is easy to grow, producing small ball-shaped flowers in yellow or white, double or single, from mid to late summer. Stems grow from a clump of scented foliage. Unfortunately the plant is not reliably hardy from Zone 5 north and should be treated as an annual.
Hardy Zones: 6-10.
Grows: 6-24" (15-60cm).
Culture: Does best in moist, fertile soils.
Spacing: 10-15" (25-38cm).

MERTENSIA VIRGINICA ◐● (Virginia Bluebells)

Tall-growing perennial producing liliac-blue or pink clusters of bell-shaped flowers during spring months. Plants are of loose open habit, making this perennial useful in natural wildflower settings.
Hardy Zones: 3-8.
Culture: Does best in moist, well-mulched soils.
Spacing: 15-18" (38-45cm).

MONARDA DIDYMA ○◐✄ (Monarda or Bee Balm)

Bee Balm is a robust perennial producing large flowers of red or pink on erect stems. Foliage emits a mint fragrance and is hairy textured. Blooming period is from early to mid summer. Cambridge Scarlet, shown above, is one of the most popular varieties, yielding scarlet-red blooms.
Hardy Zones: 4-10.
Grows: 36" (90cm).
Culture: Does best in moist organic soils.
Spacing: 12-15" (30-38cm).

BLUE WONDER CATMINT

WHITE CUPFLOWER

DWARF LILY TURF

NEPETA MUSSINII ○ ◑ ⋙
(Catmint)

A spreading perennial producing low mounds of gray-green foliage having a mint scent. From late spring to mid summer, flower spikes of blue-shaped flowers are produced. The variety Blue Wonder is somewhat more compact and flowers sky blue. Both make good edging plants.

Hardy Plants: 4-10.
Grows: 12-18" (30-45cm).
Culture: Does well in nearly any well-drained garden soil. To encourage healthy growth the following spring, a mulch of hay or straw should be applied in late autumn.
Spacing: 12-15" (30-38cm).

NIEREMBERGIA REPENS ○ ◑ ⋙
(White Cupflower)

Although Cupflowers are generally regarded as annuals from Zone 7 North, the White Cupflower can be grown as a perennial to Zone 5 if given winter protection of straw or other mulch. The White Cupflower is of creeping habit, producing white blooms from early spring to early fall.

Foliage is narrow and grasslike. Excellent plant for rock gardens.

Hardy Zones: 8-10 without protection.
Grows: 4" (10cm).
Culture: Does best in moist, but well-drained soil.
Space: 6-10" (15-25cm).

OENOTHERA FRUTICOSA 'YOUNGII' ○ ◑
(Young's Sundrops)

Although these are generally more robust-growing plants than *O. missouriensis,* they produce similar golden yellow blooms during summer months. The variety Fireworks is unique, producing reddish brown stems and buds, giving a multi-colored effect. Sometimes called *Oenothera tetragona,* Young's Sundrops and its hybrids are upright growing and do not spread. However, plants will become crowded after 2-3 years and require dividing.

Hardy Zones: 4-10.
Grows: 20" (50cm).
Culture: Does best in well-drained soil. Soil must remain

OZARK SUNDROPS

YOUNG'S SUNDROPS

well-drained during winter months.
Spacing: 15" (38cm).

OENOTHERA MISSOURIENSIS ○ ◑
(Ozark Sundrops)

Ozark Sundrops are spreading perennials bearing bright canary yellow cup-shaped flowers throughout summer months. Flowers are fragrant and are unique because they are open fullest toward early evening hours. Foliage is bright green and willowlike in appearance. Winged seed pods are tan, but often streaked with crimson. Pods are widely used in dried arrangements. Because of its trailing habit, this perennial is best used on embankments or in rock gardens. Divide every third year to avoid overcrowding.

Hardy Zones: 4-10.
Grows: 9-12" (23-30cm).
Culture: Does best in well-drained soil. Soil must remain well-drained during winter months.
Spacing: 12-15" (30-38cm).

OPHIOPOGON JAPONICUS ○ ◑
(Dwarf Lily Turf or Mondo Grass)

Dwarf Lily Turf is a creeping grasslike perennial producing lavender flowers on short stems in early summer. Blue fruits follow. This has the appearance of a clump grass. Unfortunately, it is not hardy above Zone 8. Where perennial, the plant can be left undisturbed for many years before division is necessary. This is an excellent edging or groundcover plant. Gardeners can get the same effect in northern areas by planting Liriope spicata, however.

Hardy Zones: 8-10.
Grows: 8-10" (20-25cm).
Culture: Does best in organic soils of high moisture content.
Spacing: 6-12" (15-30cm).

JAPANESE PEONY

ORIENTAL POPPY

CHINESE POPPY

PACHYSANDRA TERMINALIS ◐ ● ⌇▲
(Japanese Spurge)

Japanese Spurge is a fast-spreading groundcover, producing attractive evergreen leaves on compact stems. White flowers are produced in May. Because Pachysandra does best in partially shaded to shady locations, it makes a good groundcover under trees and shrubs.

Hardy Zones: 4-9.
Grows: 6-8" (15-20cm).
Culture: Does best in moist, but well-drained soils top dressed with bark.
Spacing: 6-12" (15-30cm).

PAEONIA LACTIFLORA ○ ◐ ✂
(Chinese Peony)

Chinese Peony is among the most popular of perennials because of its long life and dependable flowering habit. These plants produce huge, fragrant double, single, Japanese and anemone style blooms of white, red or pink shades in late spring. Plants are shrubby in appearance, making a good low hedge. Foliage is narrow. Peonies can remain undisturbed for years. Autumn is the best time to plant.

Hardy Zones: 3-8.
Grows: 30-36" (75-90cm).
Culture: Does well in nearly any garden soil except those that are continually wet.
Spacing: 24-36" (60-90cm).

PAEONIA SUFFRUTICOSA ○
(Japanese Peony)

Tree Peonies make an attractive show in perennial or shrub borders with their large blooms, produced in a wide color range including red, yellow, gold, ivory, pink, purple and often displaying golden filigreed centers. Blooms are produced in late May on plants that actually are woody shrubs. Unlike Chinese Peonies, these plants do not die down in winter months. Plant in autumn.

Hardy Zones: 3-8.
Grows: 4-5' (1.2-1.5m).
Culture: Does well in nearly any garden soil.
Spacing: 3-4' (.9-1.2m)

PAPAVER NUDICAULE ○
(Iceland Poppy)

Iceland Poppy is grown for its abundance of bloom and

JAPANESE SPURGE

BEARDSTONGUE

ICELAND POPPY

compact habit. Flowers of orange or gold are produced from late spring until late summer on thin wiry stems. Foliage is hairy and light green. Mound-shaped habit makes the plant attractive in rock gardens or as bed foreground. Best treated as a biennial, started from seed.
Hardy Zones: 2-10.
Grows: 5-10″ (12-25cm).
Culture: Does best in well-drained soils. Sow seed in spring. Will flower during summer and again the following year.
Spacing: 8-10″ (20-25cm).

PAPAVER ORIENTALIS ○
(Oriental Poppy)

Oriental Poppies are reliable perennials producing crepe paperlike blooms with attractive black stamens in May and June. Although the standard and most popular color is orange-red, a number of other shades have been added in recent years, including ivory, coral, pink, scarlet and salmon. Foliage is fernlike.
Hardy Zones: 3-8.
Grows: 36″ (90cm).

Culture: Does best in well-drained soils.
Spacing: 15-18″ (38-45cm).

PENSTEMON ○ ◐
(Beardstongue)

Most well-known of the Beardstongues are upright growers producing tubular rose or red flowers on thin 18″ (45cm) spikes during June and July. Reliable varieties include Prairie Dusk and Prairie Fire. At 12″ (30cm) are *P. barbatus* varieties including *P.b. 'Alba'* and *P.b. 'Elfin Pink'*. These also are reliably hardy and exhibit a similar growth habit. However, their compact size makes these plants more useable in small beds, borders or rock gardens. New on the scene is a spreading form named *P. × 'Crystal'*, which exhibits glossy rich green evergreen foliage and small white flower clusters in May. Foliage is neat, not long like other Penstemons.
Hardy Zones: 4-9.
Grows: 9-24″ (22-60cm).
Culture: Does best in well-drained soils.
Spacing: 12-18″ (30-45cm).

CREEPING PHLOX

TUNIC FLOWER

CHINESE LANTERN PLANT

GARDEN PHLOX

PETRORHAGIA SAXIFRAGA or *TUNICA SAXIFRAGA* ○ ⋙▲
(Tunic Flower)

Compact-growing perennial producing small pink flowers during summer months. All are good plants for rock gardens, for lining paths and as front edging to a flower border.
Hardy Zones: 4-9.
Grows: 8" (20cm).
Culture: Does well in nearly any well-drained garden soil.
Spacing: 10-12" (25-30cm).

PHLOX DECUSSATA or ○ *P. PANICULATA*
(Garden Phlox)

Phlox are often called the backbone of the perennial garden. The most widely planted varieties are from the *P. decussata* family. These are robust plants with large panicles of small florets produced in nearly every color of the rainbow. Some have distinct eyes that contrast nicely with floret color. Blooms are scented and produced freely throughout the summer months.

Hardy Zones: 3-9.
Grows: 2-4' (60-120cm).
Culture: Does best in moist soil rich in organic matter.
Spacing: 18" (45cm).

PHLOX SUBULATA ○ ⋙▲
(Creeping Phlox)

Dwarf creeping perennial producing showy masses of small flowers in white, blue and rose shades during early spring. Foliage is needle-shaped and evergreen. Good plant for hillside and rock garden plantings. Plants spread rapidly and roots bind soil to prevent erosion.
Hardy Zones: 3-9.
Grows: 4-5" (10-12cm).
Culture: Does best in well-drained garden soils.
Spacing: 8-12" (20-30cm).

PHYSALIS FRANCHETII ○✂
(Chinese Lantern Plant)

This perennial is primarily grown for its ornamental orange seed pods that resemble miniature Chinese lanterns. Small white flowers are produced in early summer,

PINK FALSE DRAGONHEAD

VIVID FALSE DRAGONHEAD

MARIES BALLOON FLOWER

WHITE BALLOON FLOWER

with seed pods appearing in August. Plants are vigorous, needing room to spread. Lantern seed pods are snipped in early autumn to be used in dried bouquets.
Hardy Zones: 3-10.
Grows: 18" (45cm).
Culture: Does well in nearly any garden soil.
Spacing: 24" (60cm).

PHYSOSTEGIA VIRGINIANA ○ ◑ ✂
(False Dragonhead)

False Dragonhead is a medium-growing perennial producing long spikes of tubular flowers in late summer and early fall. Most popular color is pink, but recently white and orchid-pink have been added to the color range. Vivid, at 20" (50cm), is a new compact growing variety producing large orchid-pink flowers. A new white is Summer Snow, producing blooms 3 weeks ahead of other varieties. It grows 30" (75cm). All Physostegias have willowlike dark green foliage. Plants are vigorous, so dividing every 2-3 years should be done to avoid overcrowding.
Hardy Zones: 3-10.

Grows: 20-48" (50-120cm).
Culture: Does well in nearly any garden soil.
Spacing: 15-18" (38-45cm).

PLATYCODON GRANDIFLORA ○ ◑
(Balloon Flower)

Balloon flowers are reliable perennials that get their name from buds that swell into miniature balloons before opening. Cuplike blooms are produced throughout the summer in white, blue and pink, although blue is predominate. Although most varieties grow nearly 2 feet (60cm), *P.g. 'Mariesii'* is a violet blue compact grower at 12-15" (30-38cm). Short and tall varieties are reliable performers in border or rock garden situations. Little maintenance is required to keep plants looking attractive from season to season.
Hardy Zones: 3-10.
Grows: 12-24" (30-60cm).
Culture: Does best in well-drained garden soils.
Spacing: 12-18" (30-45cm).

LEADWORT

SOLOMON SEAL

JACOB'S LADDER

PLUMBAGO LARPENTAE or CERATOSTIGMA PLUMBAGINOIDES ○ ◑ ∿
(Leadwort)

Leadwort is a trouble free groundcover that produces small blue flowers from midsummer to early autumn. The plant's dark green foliage takes on a reddish hue during late fall. Leadwort spreads through growth in its root system, making it ideal for preventing soil erosion.
Hardy Zones: 5-10.
Grows: 8-12" (20-30cm).
Culture: Does best in well-drained soils.
Spacing: 18-24" (45-60cm).

POLEMONIUM CAERULEUM ○✂
(Jacob's Ladder)

Beautiful perennial producing light blue flowers in April and May. Foliage is fernlike in appearance. Gaining popularity against the standard form is Blue Pearl, which is more compact growing. Both are good cut flowers and attractive in the flower border.
Hardy Zones: 2-8.
Grows: 12-15" (30-38cm).

Culture: Does best in moist, but well-drained soils rich in organic matter.
Spacing: 18" (45cm).

POLYGONATUM COMMUTATUM ◑
(Solomon Seal)

Solomon Seal is a tall-growing perennial with arching stems producing long silvery green leaves. Small bell-shaped flowers of white or yellow-green are produced in spring. Although reputed to grow 6 ft. (1.8m) it is unusual to see specimens in the wild or cultivated half this size. This is an attractive plant for the wildgarden.
Hardy Zones: 3-10.
Grows: 36" (90cm).
Culture: Does best in moist soil high in organic matter.
Spacing: 12-15" (30-38cm).

POLYGONUM REYNOUTRIA ○ ∿
(Japanese Fleece Flower or Dwarf Lace Plant)

Dense groundcover producing pink flowers in late summer. Plants have spreading habit and often reach 24" (60cm) in height the second year. Foliage is bright green.

BETHLEHEM SAGE

JAPANESE FLEECE FLOWER or DWARF LACE PLANT

CINQUEFOIL

A dwarf named Border Jewel is very attractive, making a good low groundcover or edging. It produces fleecy pink flowers in May.
Hardy Zones: 2-8.
Grows: 5-24" (12-60cm).
Culture: Does well in well-drained garden soil. Should be sheared each spring to ensure vigorous new growth.
Spacing: 18" (45cm).

POTENTILLA VAR. ○ ◑ ⋙ ▲
(Cinquefoil)

Most gardeners are familiar with the shrubby Cinquefoils, but many are not aware of the useful perennial ground-cover types that can add immeasurably to the attractive-ness of a rock garden or flower border. Perhaps the most popular is *P. aurea verna,* with lush green strawberrylike foliage and producing bright yellow flowers from June to mid July. This plant is a mat former with trailing stems. Related is *P. villosa.* Foliage has a woolly appearance. The plant produces bright yellow flowers in May-June. Another creeper is *P. tonguei,* producing evergreen foli-age and unusual apricot colored blooms with crimson

centers. None of these grow more than 3" (7.5cm). In contrast is the more upright growing form, *P. nepalensis,* of which Miss Wilmott is the most widely propagated variety. Miss Wilmott flowers carmine-red in June and July and attains a height of 12" (30cm).
Hardy Zones: 4-9.
Grows: 3-12" (7.5-30cm).
Culture: Does well in well-drained garden soil.
Spacing: 10-12" (25-30cm).

PULMONARIA SACCHARATA ◑
(Bethlehem Sage)

This spring flowering perennial produces pink flowers that turn blue as they mature. Foliage is narrow, silvery green and has white spots. Related is Blue lungwort, *P. angustifolia.* These produce drooping clusters of blue, pink or white trumpet-shaped blooms, depending on variety, from spring to early summer. Both are attractive in a shady corner of the flower border.
Hardy Zones: 3-9.
Grows: 8-12" (20-30cm).
Culture: Does best in moist, highly organic soils.
Spacing: 10" (25cm).

PRIMROSE

PURPLE CONEFLOWER

BLACK-EYED SUSAN

PRIMULA VAR. ◖✕
(Primrose)

Primroses are attractive border or rock garden plants requiring moist, but well-drained organic soils and partial shade. Nearly all perennial forms are identified by their rich green leaves produced in a rosette at the plant's base. Flowers, produced in a wide range of styles, are borne on stalks devoid of foliage. Becoming more popular in recent years have been the *P. polyantha* types, particularly members of the Giant strain, blooming in white, rose, red, scarlet, purple, lavender and yellow. Plants are compact and floral clusters nearly cover plants April-June. These plants receive part of their parentage from the English Primrose, *P. vulgaris,* another compact-growing form, producing single or double flowers of yellow, pink, red, apricot, blue and purple. Also of low stature are Auricula Primroses, bearing scented clusters of small white, red, purple, blue-rose or copper flowers in May. Completing the list of low growers are *P. veris* and *P. elatior,* both producing evergreen foliage and large flower heads in yellow tones. In recent years, however, the *P. veris* color range has been expanded to include

copper, red, and purple shades. Varieties growing to 12" (30cm) or more include *P. denticulata,* the Himalayan Primrose, producing large globe-shaped floral heads of tiny flowers of purple, rose or red shades. Completing the range of perennial Primroses are the candelabra types, growing to 24" (60cm). One of the more popular is *P. japonica* producing rose, white, pink, or red blooms in rings around and on top of the stalk.
Hardy Zones: 4-8.
Grows: 6-24" (15-60cm).
Culture: Do well in moist, but well-drained soils high in organic matter. *P. japonica,* however, needs continually moist soil.
Spacing: 6-12" (15-30cm).

RUDBECKIA FULGIDA ◯◖✕
(Black-Eyed Susan)

Coneflowers are tall-growing perennials producing long-lasting golden yellow flowers with dark centers. Popular is the variety Goldsturm that flowers from midsummer to midautumn. Blooms have long petals and sooty black centers; foliage is narrow and silvery green. Goldquelle is a spectacular double flowering variety producing gold-

BLOOD VEIN SAGE

HERB OF GRACE

BLUE SAGE

en yellow blooms during the same period as Goldsturm.
Hardy Zones: 3-10.
Grows: 24-30" (60-75cm).
Culture: Does best in well-drained soil.
Spacing: 12-15" (30-38cm).

RUDBECKIA PURPUREA or ECHINACEA PURPUREA ○✕ (Purple Coneflower)

These perennials are similar in habit to *Rudbeckia fulgida,* producing large ray-shaped blooms, but in lavender-red with purple centers. The variety Bright Star displays even larger blooms than the standard. Blooms are rosy red and have maroon centers. A white form with bronze centers is also available.
Hardy Zones: 3-10.
Grows: 30-36" (75-90cm).
Culture: Does best in well-drained soil.
Spacing: 18-24" (45-60cm).

RUTA GRAVEOLENS ○ ◗ (Herb of Grace)

This is a perennial aromatic herb grown for its decorative

mound of blue-green foliage. Small yellow flowers are produced in summer months. A staple in the herb garden, this plant is also finding use in the perennial border.
Hardy Zones: 4-9.
Grows: 18" (45cm).
Culture: Does best in well-drained soil.
Spacing: 18" (45cm).

SALVIA VAR. ○ (Meadow Sage)

Meadow Sage is the name loosely applied to perennial forms of Salvia encompassing: *S. azurea; S. haematodes; S. pitcheri;* and *S. virgata nemerosa.* Although each bears blue or purple flowers, overall appearance among forms is quite different. *S. azurea,* or Blue Sage, is a tall-growing type producing spikes of sky blue flowers in late summer and fall. Similar in habit to Blue Sage is *S. pitcheri,* although flowers are of deeper blue. Bloodvein Sage, *S. haematodes* produces stalks bearing lavender-blue flowers and unusual gray-green foliage with blood-red veins. Violet sage is the common name of *S. nemerosa virgata.*

COMMON SAGE

LAVENDER COTTON

VIOLET SAGE

East Friesland is the most widely grown variety producing lavender spikes from early to mid summer.
Hardy Zones: 5-10.
Grows: 18-48" (45-120cm).
Culture: Does best in well-drained soil.
Spacing: 15-18" (38-45cm).

SALVIA OFFICINALIS ○
(Common Sage)

Sage is an attractive perennial for flower border or herb garden. Foliage is silvery blue and flower spikes, produced in late spring into early summer, are lavender. Foliage emits a sweet fragrance. Another form is *S.o. 'Aurea',* with leaves a golden hue. Both forms are reliable once established. Some of the many uses as an herb are listed on page 96. Plants are noted for their ability to withstand droughty conditions.

Hardy Zones: 3-10.
Grows: 24" (60cm).
Culture: Does well in nearly any well-drained garden soil.
Spacing: 18-24" (45-60cm).

SALVIA SUPERBA ○
(Violet Sage)

Violet Sage is an attractive perennial for the flower border producing long spikes of ½" (1.2cm) violet blooms in June and July. Plants are shrubby and reliable.
Hardy Zones: 3-10.
Grows: 24-30" (60-75cm).
Culture: Does well in well-drained garden soil.
Spacing: 18" (45cm).

SANTOLINA INCANA ○ ⋙♠
(Lavender Cotton)

This aromatic herb produces silver-gray woolly foliage. It is widely used as an edging plant or in rock gardens. Small round yellow flowers are produced in June. At maturity, the plant is shrublike in appearance, growing nearly as wide as it does tall.

Hardy Zones: 5-10.
Grows: 12-18" (30-45cm).
Culture: Does best in well-drained soil. Needs to be clip-

PINCUSHION FLOWER

GREEN LAVENDER COTTON

NEAPOLITAN LAVENDER COTTON

ped after flowering and pruned heavily in early spring to perform well.
Spacing: 18-24" (45-60cm).

SANTOLINA NEAPOLITANA ○ ᗯ▲
(Neapolitan Lavender Cotton)

Compact-growing, aromatic perennial producing silvery foliage on pendulous branches. The graceful plants are shrubby in appearance and widely used in low borders or as edging. Yellow buttonlike flowers are produced in June and July.
Hardy Zones: 7-10.
Grows: 12-15" (30-38cm).
Culture: Does best in well-drained garden soil.
Spacing: 15" (38cm).

SANTOLINA VIRENS ○ ᗯ▲
(Green Lavender Cotton)

This plant is another shrubby perennial producing emerald-green foliage and yellow buttonlike flowers in June. Foliage is aromatic. Plants are widely used in low

borders or edging, often in combination with silvery leaved Santolinas.
Hardy Zones: 7-10.
Grows: 12" (30cm).
Culture: Does best in well-drained garden soil.
Spacing: 15" (38cm).

SCABIOSA CAUCASICA ○✄
(Pincushion Flower)

Pincushion flower is a late summer flowering perennial. Blooms resemble pin cushions and colors include shades of blue, white, mauve, lavender and violet. Foliage is gray-green. This is an attractive perennial for the flower border and prized as a cut flower.
Hardy Zones: 3-10.
Grows: 18-24" (45-60cm).
Culture: Does best in well-drained soils of alkaline pH.
Spacing: 12-15" (30-38cm).

HENS AND CHICKS (MIXED)

SOAPWORT

PRAIRIE MALLOW or MINIATURE HOLLYHOCK

SAPONARIA OCYMOIDES ○ ⋙ ✄
(Soapwort)

Soapwort is a low-growing spreading perennial with semi-evergreen foliage and bright pink flowers in May and June. The compact, mounded plants are vigorous matformers, useful as groundcover and attractive in rock gardens. Plants perform much the same function as the earlier flowering perennial *Phlox subulata*.

Hardy Zones: 2-9.
Grows: 6″ (15cm).
Culture: Does well in nearly any garden soil.
Spacing: 15-18″ (38-45cm).

SEMPERVIVUM HYBRIDS ○ ⋙ ▲
(Hens and Chicks)

Hens and Chicks are attractive low-growing succulents with fleshy leaves in red and green shades. Some have cobweb appearing growth and all feature rosettes with many offsets. These are excellent plants for rock gardens, flower borders and containers. Varieties are too numerous to mention.

Hardy Zones: 4-10.

Grows: 4-6″ (10-15″).
Culture: Does best in well-drained soils and can tolerate droughty conditions.
Spacing: 8-10″ (20-25cm).

SENECIO TYROLENSIS ○
(Groundsel)

This compact-growing perennial produces evergreen foliage and yellow clusters of daisylike flowers in May. Makes an attractive rock garden plant.

Hardy Zones: 4-9.
Grows: 8″ (20cm).
Culture: Does best in well-drained soils.
Spacing: 8-10″ (20-25cm).

SIDALCEA HYBRIDS ○ ✄
(Prairie Mallow or Miniature Hollyhock)

Although resembling the giant annual Hollyhock, Prairie Mallow is not a member of the same family. This perennial produces small papery cup-shaped blooms in pink, red, purple or white during June and July. Bloom period can be extended however, if faded flowers are picked. Re-

COBWEB HENS AND CHICKS

GOLDENROD

LAMB'S EARS or WOOLLY BETONY

moving spent blooms can extend flowering until autumn. Foliage is almost palmlike in appearance, covering stalks to the plant's base. Prairie Mallow is attractive in the flower border, wildgarden and good for cutting.

Hardy Zones: 5-10.
Grows: 36" (90cm).
Culture: Does best in well-drained soil.
Spacing: 15-18" (38-45cm).

SOLIDOLGO HYBRIDS ○✂
(Goldenrod)

The hybrid Goldenrods are excellent border plants providing splashy sprays of golden yellow blooms from late summer to early autumn. Two major varieties are in common supply, the 36" (90cm) Goldenmosa and 12" (30cm) Golden Dwarf. Large golden sprays and attractive foliage with yellow highlights make the larger version attractive for cut bouquets.

Hardy Zones: 3-9.
Grows: 12-36" (30-90cm).
Culture: Does well in nearly any well-drained garden soil.
Spacing: 12-15" (30-38cm).

STACHYS LANATA ○
(Lamb's Ears or Woolly Betony)

Although this perennial produces spikes of purple blossoms in early summer, the plant is grown primarily for its silvery white tongue-shaped woolly textured foliage. With spikes, the plant can grow 18-24" (45-60cm). However, a new hybrid named Silver Carpet is now available that does not bloom and grows to just 12" (30cm), making the plant useful as a groundcover, not merely an accent in the perennial border.

Hardy Zones: 3-10.
Grows: 10-24" (25-60cm).
Culture: Does best in well-drained garden soil.
Spacing: 12-15" (30-38cm).

GOLDEN CARPET or GOLD MOSS

WHITE STONECROP

ELLACOMBIANUM STONECROP

SEDUM or STONECROP

Most Sedum varieties are groundcovers that perform best in dry soils and full sun. All have fleshy leaves and produce unusual flowers. Some of the more common types are described below:

SEDUM ACRE ○ ᨠ
(Golden Carpet or Gold Moss)
Low-growing, spreading plant producing yellow flowers in early summer. Good mat former for the rock garden in areas receiving no traffic.
Hardy Zones: 3-10.
Grows: 3-6" (7.5-15cm).
Culture: Does best in well-drained soils and can tolerate droughty conditions.
Spacing: 9-12" (24-30cm).

SEDUM ALBUM ○ ᨠ
(White Stonecrop)
Low-growing, spreading succulent producing white flowers in midsummer. Dense mat of semi-evergreen foliage turns pink-red in autumn.
Hardy Zones: 3-10.

Grows: 3-4" (7.5-10cm).
Culture: Does best in well-drained soils and can tolerate droughty conditions.
Spacing: 9-12" (24-30cm).

SEDUM ELLACOMBIANUM ○ ᨠ
(Ellacombianum Stonecrop)
Groundcover type sedum producing mounds of lemon-yellow flowers during June. Attractive green club shaped foliage is produced in summer and fall.
Hardy Zones: 3-10.
Grows: 6-8" (15-20cm).
Culture: Does best in well-drained soils and can tolerate droughty conditions.
Spacing: 9-12" (24-30cm).

SEDUM KAMTSCHATICUM ○ ᨠ
(Kamtschaticum Stonecrop)
Spreading stonecrop producing yellow-orange flowers starting in late spring continuing through late summer. Foliage an attractive dark green and scalloped. Variegated form is also available. Foliage is light green tinged with pink.

OCTOBER PLANT

METEOR STONECROP

OREGANUM STONECROP

KAMTSCHATICUM STONECROP

Hardy Zones: 3-10.
Grows: 3-4" (7.5-10cm).
Culture: Does best in well-drained soils.
Spacing: 9-12" (24-30cm).

SEDUM OREGANUM GLAUCUM ○ ⋙
(Oreganum Stonecrop)

Clump-growing sedum with fat fleshy leaves of a brilliant emerald color. White flowers are produced in late spring.
Hardy Zones: 3-10.
Grows: 2-3" (5-7.5cm).
Culture: Does best in well-drained soils.
Spacing: 6-9" (15-24cm).

SEDUM SIEBOLDII ○ ⋙
(October Plant)

Trailing form producing pink floral heads in early autumn. Foliage an attractive slate green. An attractive plant for rock gardens and when potted up as a houseplant.
Hardy Zones: 3-10.
Grows: 6-10" (15-25cm).
Culture: Grows best in well-drained soils.

Spacing: 15-18" (38-45cm).

SEDUM SPATHULIFOLIUM ○ ⋙

This form of Stonecrop is low growing, producing fat globular silver-green leaves. Petite yellow flowers are borne on short stems in June and July. Like other Sedum varieties, it is a good plant for the rock garden or other areas where soil is poor and somewhat droughty.
Hardy Zones: 3-10.
Grows: 3-4" (7.5-10cm).
Culture: Does best in well-drained soil. Tolerates infertile conditions.
Spacing: 6" (15cm).

SEDUM SPECTABILE VAR. ○
(Showy Stonecrop)

One of the taller-growing sedums producing large flat clusters of tiny red, pink or ivory colored florets in late summer to frost. Gray-green foliage is fleshy. Autumn Joy and Brilliant are popular varieties.
Hardy Zones: 3-10.
Grows: 18" (45cm).
Culture: Grows best in well-drained soils.
Spacing: 18-24" (45-60cm).

SPATHULIFOLIUM SEDUM

DRAGON'S BLOOD SEDUM

STOKE'S ASTER

SEDUM SPURIUM 'DRAGON'S BLOOD' ◯ ⋙
(Dragon's Blood Sedum)

Dragon's Blood is a low-growing sedum producing intense red flowers from June through August. It makes a spreading carpet that is easy to maintain. Similar forms include Bronze Carpet, with pink flowers and *S.s. 'Coccineum',* producing bright rose-pink blooms. All have fleshy leaves that are bronze-green.
Hardy Zones: 3-10.
Grows: 3-4" (7.5-10cm).
Culture: Does best in well-drained soil. Tolerates infertile conditions.
Spacing: 9-12" (22-30cm).

SOLIDASTER LUTEUS ◯ ✄
(Solidaster)

This perennial is a cross between the aster and goldenrod. Goldenrod contributed to the bright golden yellow color and aster parentage is responsible for the flowers starlike shape. Shrubby plants bloom from midsummer until early autumn. Solidaster often grows twice in diameter its mature height. Because of its vigorous, spreading

habit, division is necessary after 2-3 years to prevent overcrowding. Plants are attractive in the flower border and blooms cut well.
Hardy Zones: 5-10.
Grows: 18-24" (45-60cm).
Culture: Does best in well-drained soil.
Spacing: 15-18" (38-45cm).

STOKESIA LAEVIS ◯ ✄
(Stoke's Aster)

Stoke's Aster is attractive in the perennial border and as a cut flower. It produces large blue asterlike flower heads, one to a stalk, from July until frost. Foliage is shiny and narrow, ranging from 2-8" (5-20cm) long. Four varieties are widespread. Most compact is Blue Danube, a deep blue, which is similar to another deep blue variety, Wyoming. Taller varieties include Cyanea, with larger than average blue blooms and Silver Moon, a white variety.
Hardy Zones: 5-10.
Grows: 12-18" (30-45cm).
Culture: Does best in well drained soil.
Spacing: 12-15" (30-38cm).

CAUCASIAN COMFREY

GERMANDER

HIDCOTE COMFREY

SYMPHYTUM CAUCASICUM &
S. GRANDIFLORUM 'HIDCOTE' ○
(Comfrey)

Comfrey is an easily grown perennial of coarse, open habit. Plants have long, lance-shaped heavily veined leaves. *S. caucasicum* produces red-purple flowers that turn blue as they mature. The bell-shaped blooms continue to open from June to mid-August. Flowering at about the same time is *S.g. 'Hidcote'*, producing pale blooms with a pink cast. Both are good plants for the wildgarden or near a body of water.
Hardy Zones: 5-9.
Grows: 18-24″ (45-60cm).
Culture: Does best in moist soil.
Spacing: 12-15″ (30-38cm).

TEUCRIUM CHAMAEDRYS &
T. CHAMAEDRYS PROSTRATUM ○▲
(Germander)

The Germanders are shrubby plants that can be used as groundcover or low hedging. Both forms produce ever-green foliage with a glossy sheen and rosy pink to lilac flowers during June and July. However, *T. chamaedrys prostratum,* often called *T. canadense,* is rapid spreading and makes the best groundcover because of its compact habit. This Germander can take foot traffic and growth density can be made thicker if sheared soon after flowering. The standard Germander makes a neat boxwoodlike hedge, withstanding pruning well to 12″ (30cm). Although both forms do well in full sun, *T. chamaedrys prostratum* tolerates shady locations.
Hardy Zones: 5-10.
Grows: 6-15″ (15-38cm).
Culture: Does best in well-drained soil.
Spacing: 6-12″ (15-30cm).

MEADOW RUE

FALSE LUPINE

LEMON THYME

MOTHER OF THYME

THALICTRUM AQUILEGIFOLIUM ○ ◑ ✂
(Meadow Rue)

Tall-growing perennial producing large panicles of soft pink-purple flowers in June and July. Good plant for near the back of a flower border. Foliage and blooms attractive in cut flower bouquets.
Hardy Zones: 4-9.
Grows: 36" (90cm).
Culture: Does best in moist soils high in organic matter. Needs winter mulching Zone 5 and north.
Spacing: 15-18" (38-45cm).

THERMOPSIS CAROLINIANA ○ ✂
(False Lupine)

Long-lived perennial producing large spikes of yellow blossoms in June and July. Plants are tall and broad spreading. Flowers are good for cutting. Plants make a showy display in the back of the perennial border.
Hardy Zones: 4-9.
Grows: 3-4' (.9-1.2m).
Culture: Does best in fertile, well-drained soil.
Spacing: 3-4' (.9-1.2m).

THYMUS × CITRIODORUS ○ ⋘ ▲
(Lemon Thyme)

This delightful subshrub or evergreen herb produces light green lemon-scented foliage. New growth is gold. However, the cultivar *T.c. 'Aureus'* retains its gold color through most of the growing season. Other well known cultivars include *T.c. 'Argentea'* and *T.c. 'Silver Queen'*. All produce small pink flowers in June and July. Plants are excellent as bed foreground, in rock and herb gardens.
Hardy Zones: 4-10.
Grows: 12" (30cm).
Culture: Does best in warm, well-drained soils.
Spacing: 10-12" (25-30cm).

THYMUS SERPYLLUM ○ ◑ ⋘
(Mother of Thyme)

Rapidly spreading evergreen herb widely used as groundcover or in the rock garden. Produces small aromatic evergreen leaves and long trailing stems that root as they spread. Tiny purple flowers are borne in summer months.

84

PERIWINKLE

GLOBE FLOWER

BIGLEAF PERIWINKLE

VIRGINIA SPIDERWORT

Hardy Zones: 3-10.
Grows: 2-6" (5-15cm).
Culture: Does best in warm, well-drained soils.
Spacing: 6-12" (15-30cm).

TRADESCANTIA VIRGINIANA ○ ◑
(Virginia Spiderwort)

Another reliable perennial producing three-lobed blooms in white, blue, purple and rose-red from late spring to midsummer. Foliage is grasslike in appearance. During bloom period, needs frequent pruning to maintain neat appearance.
Hardy Zones: 4-10.
Grows: 18" (45cm).
Culture: Does best in moist, organic soil.
Spacing: 12-15" (30-38cm).

TROLLIUS LEDEBOURI ○ ◑ ✂
(Globe Flower)

Producer of large buttercuplike blooms, ranging from golden yellow to orange, from late spring to late summer. Good plant for the back of a flower border. Flowers attractive in mixed cut bouquets.

Hardy Zones: 3-9.
Grows: 36" (90cm).
Culture: Requires a moist soil rich in organic matter.
Spacing: 10-12" (25-30cm).

VINCA MAJOR and *V. MINOR* ○ ◑ ● ⌇ ♠
(Perwinkle or Trailing Myrtle)

Popular groundcovers with evergreen foliage and woody stems producing blue-purple flowers in late spring. Particularly useful under shrubs, trees and on embankments where little else will survive. Bowles is a *V. minor* variety having larger leaves than the standard. However, *Vinca major* foliage is twice as large and lighter green, although spreading no more rapidly.
Hardy Zones: 4-10.
Grows: 6" (15cm).
Culture: Does well in average garden soils.
Spacing: 12" (30cm).

TUFTED PANSY

BLUE MARSH VIOLA

SWEET VIOLET

VERBENA VENOSA ○ ∿
(Hardy Verbena)

This low-growing, mat-forming perennial produces globe-shaped flower heads bearing tiny flowers in red, rose, violet, or purple throughout the summer months. Foliage is narrow and heavily veined. Spread often reaches 24" (60cm) in diameter. Because the plant is only semi-hardy, it needs a winter mulch of straw.
Hardy Zones: 5-9.
Grows: 4" (10cm).
Culture: Does well in average garden soil.
Spacing: 18-24" (45-60cm).

VERONICA LATIFOLIA 'CRATER LAKE' ○ ◑ ✂
(Crater Lake Hungarian Speedwell)

Crater Lake Blue Speedwell is widely planted because of its reliable performance, gentian-blue flowers and compact habit. Flowers are produced in June through August on 15" (38cm) stems. The plant is attractive in the flower border, rock garden and on embankments.
Hardy Zones: 3-10.
Grows: 15" (38cm).

Culture: Does best in well-drained garden soils.
Spacing: 12-15" (30-38cm).

VERONICA LONGIFOLIA ○ ◑
(Spike Speedwell)

Spike Speedwell is an attractive border perennial producing long spikes of pink or blue flowers from midsummer until fall. Plants are bushy and produce long narrow saw toothed leaves. Minuet and Pavane are good pink forms. *V.l. subsessilis* produces violet-blue flowers, but is nearly twice as tall at 36" (90cm).
Hardy Zones: 3-10.
Grows: 18-36" (45-90cm).
Culture: Does best in well-drained garden soils.
Spacing: 15-18" (38-45cm).

VIOLA CORNUTA ○ ◑ ✂
(Tufted Pansy)

The Tufted Pansy is a spreading, compact-growing perennial producing blue, white or lavender flowers from April to frost. However, there are some bicolors coming onto the market. Established is Purple Glory, a violet bloomer

HARDY VERBENA

SPIKE SPEEDWELL

CRATER LAKE SPEEDWELL

with yellow eye. Foliage is glossy and heart-shaped.
Hardy Zones: 4-8.
Grows: 5-8" (13-20cm).
Culture: Does best in sandy, well-drained soil.
Spacing: 10-12" (25-30cm).

VIOLA CUCULLATA ○ ◑ ✂
(Blue Marsh Viola)

This is a lush-growing perennial producing large heart-shaped leaves and small pansy-shaped flowers. Although the predominant color is blue, white, violet, lavender and bicolors are now available. This is not a spreading form of viola, yet the plant makes an attractive groundcover when planted close together.
Hardy Zones: 4-9.
Grows: 6-8" (15-20cm).
Culture: Does best in continually moist soils.
Spacing: 10-12" (25-30cm).

VIOLA ODORATA ○ ◑ ✂
(Sweet Violet)

Varieties of *V. odorata* are now available in an expanding range of colors. Blooms are fragrant, showy and foliage is large and heart-shaped. Blooms are similar to, but smaller than annual pansies, and appear in April and May. Like other members of the Viola family, it suffers in summer heat when the need for shady soils high in moisture content is most critical.

Three of the more popular varieties include Red Giant, red; Royal Robe, violet; and White Czar, white. These are creeping, useful perennials widely found as edging and bed foreground.
Hardy Zones: 4-9.
Grows: 6-8 (15-20cm).
Culture: Requires moist, organic soil.
Spacing: 15-18" (38-45cm).

VERONICA PROSTRATA

ADAM'S NEEDLE

PINK SPIKE SPEEDWELL

BLUE SPIKE SPEEDWELL

VERONICA PROSTRATA ○ ◐ ⋙

V. prostrata varieties are most often taller than Creeping Speedwell and exhibit narrow grassy foliage. Flowers are produced on short spikes of lilac, gentian and dark blue during May and June. *V. prostrata* spreads, making an ideal groundcover for sunny, well-drained locations.
Hardy Zones: 5-9.
Grows: 4-10" (10-25cm).
Culture: Does best in warm, well-drained soils.
Spacing: 12" (30cm).

VERONICA REPENS ○ ◐ ⋙
(Creeping Speedwell)

Creeping Speedwell is a low-growing mat former producing clusters of small blue, white or pink flowers during spring months. Foliage is shiny green, making a neat appearance throughout the growing season. North of Zone 9, it dies back in winter months, reappearing the following spring. Because of its rapid spreading habit, Creeping Speedwell makes a good groundcover.
Hardy Zones: 5-9.
Grows: 4" (10cm).
Culture: Does best in moist, but well-drained soils. Bark mulch should be used to protect shallow roots from moisture stress.
Spacing: 12" (30cm).

VERONICA SPICATA ○ ◐
(Spike Speedwell)

Spike Speedwell is a showy perennial, producing long spikes of white, pink or lavender flowers throughout the summer months. Foliage is produced near the base of the plant which is narrow and having saw tooth edges. At 18-20" (45-50cm), Minuet and Pavane are reliable pink varieties, while Icicle is white. More compact in habit are Red and Blue Fox. All are attractive accent plants.
Hardy Zones: 3-10.
Grows: 15-20" (38-50cm).
Culture: Does best in well-drained soil.
Spacing: 12-15" (30-38cm).

YUCCA FILAMENTOSA ○ ▲
(Adam's Needle)

Yucca finds best use outside the flower garden or border, usually as a specimen combined with shrubs, groundcover and decorative stone. The plant produces a large basal clump of lance-shaped leaves, above which stately spikes of white flowers grow, blooming in midsummer. Foliage is evergreen. Another widely used variety is *Y. glauca,* with narrower deep blue foliage with white margins. Floral spikes are shorter and blooms are ivory.
Hardy Zones: 4-10. (*Y. glauca* 3-10.)
Grows: 3-5' (.9-1.5m).
Culture: Does best in well-drained soil.
Spacing: 24" (60cm).

PERENNIAL BORDER FEATURING OZARK SUNDROPS IN FOREGROUND, RED HOT POKER (TRITOMA), CENTER, AND FOXGLOVE PROVIDING BACKGROUND.

PAMPAS GRASS

Combining Perennials with Ornamental Grasses

Ornamental grasses are becoming more widely used around the home and in commercial landscapes because of their relatively low maintenance and interesting foliage that contrasts nicely with that of shrubs and flowering perennials.

These grasses range from less than 12" (30cm) to varieties growing 10' (3m) or more. A number of these grasses are extremely hardy, providing beauty to the garden throughout the year.

The use of ornamental grasses originated in the Orient. Yet, their uses today are little different than those employed by ancient Far East gardeners. Clump or mound styles are useful as bed edging, accents in a rock garden or as a groundcover. One of the most widely planted of this type is Blue Fescue, *Festuca ovina glauca,* which grows 10-12" (25-30cm). It produces stiff, narrow blue blades radiating from the plant's base. *F.o.g. 'Sea Urchin'*

is an improved form with foliage intense blue and growth even more compact than the species.

Of similar habit, but producing wider foliage of a cascading nature, is Orchard Grass, *Dactylis lutea.* This is attractive in the garden because of ivory variegation along foliage margins, which contrasts well with its lush green midribs. Orchard Grass is somewhat more robust than Blue Fescue, reaching a mature height of 12-15" (30-37cm). It is also known for tolerance of shaded planting sites.

Rose Fountain Grass, *Pennisetum alopecuroides,* is a compact-growing ornamental producing long fluffy plumes of silvery rose borne from mid to late summer. This is a good accent grass in the perennial garden and despite its 2' (60cm) height, stalks are widely used in dried flower arrangements.

One of the more widely known mid range grasses is Maiden Grass, *Miscanthus sinensis 'Gracillimus',* reaching 4-5' (1.2-1.5m). Ornamental grasses in this height range are widely used near the back of a border, with shrubs, and prized for dried arrangements. Maiden Grass produces rich green foliage and tall spikes of feathery

LILY TURF

BLUE FESCUE

ORCHARD GRASS

fine textured creamy white flowers. If left in the garden over winter, foliage and plumes turn an attractive golden color.

In this same height range is Variegated Fountain Grass, *Miscanthus sinensis 'Zebrinus'*. It is harder to find than *M.s. 'Gracillimus'*, but spectacular with gold and green stripes. Feathery pink and beige plumes are produced in late summer. Variegated Fountain Grass is tolerant of some shade and does well in damp locations, making it valuable near ponds or low areas of the garden.

Another moisture lover is Glyceria, *Glyceria aquatica 'Variegata'*. This ornamental produces smooth arching leaves that are green striped with yellow. Early shoots have pink undersides. Creamy spikes are produced above the foliage in late summer. Of similar habit is Ribbon Grass, *Phalaris arundinacea variegata picta*. This ornamental grows to 5' (1.5m), with arching foliage green with white variegation.

Tallest of the perennial grasses is Pampas Grass, *Cortaderia selloana,* growing 8-10' (2.4-3m). This grass produces large plumes of creamy white or rose in September and October above narrow foliage. Unfortunately,

Pampas Grass is not hardy above Zone 7 and is best treated as an annual in northern gardens. It is often used as a specimen in the landscape and provides a good background for shorter flowering perennials. Plumes are in wide demand for dried arrangements.

Although the common name suggests it to be a grass, Lily Turf, *Liriope spicata,* is a flowering perennial. Yet, it also can provide the same function as some of the low-growing grasses.

Lily Turf is attractive as a border edging or accent in the rock garden. It also makes a good groundcover, which does well in either sun or shade. Pale violet to white flowers are produced above the grasslike foliage in July and August. Blue blackberry-like fruit appears in autumn. Mature height is 12" (30cm).

Although two ornamental grasses were mentioned as being tolerant of damp soils, the vast majority need a well-drained location. Mulching in winter will help assure vigorous growth the following spring. Tall varieties should be cut in early spring to spur new growth.

INTERRUPTED FERN

LADY FERN

MARSH MARIGOLD

FAWNLILY

INTRODUCING WILDFLOWERS INTO PERENNIAL PLANTINGS

Although wildflowers are generally thought of as being very particular regarding habitat, there are a number that adapt well to a garden environment.

As a result, these native plants are being incorporated into borders, rock gardens and naturalized plantings in the home landscape. Plants, bulbs or seeds are available, depending on kinds chosen.

In the border, wildflowers can take the place of perennials. Select these according to cultural requirements, height and flowering time. Therefore, the method for selecting wildflowers will be similar to choosing domestic varieties.

Rock garden plantings involve choosing species that work well with perennials 12″ (30cm) or less. Again, the object is to spread the season of bloom and select planting sites that are similar to each plant's native habitat. A number of these wildflowers are cliff dwellers, so they work well when pressed into rockwall crevasses or planted between boulders and along gravel paths.

Where possible, it is good to plant wildflowers in natural settings. These areas may include stream banks, under trees or shrubs, covering an embankment or along a forest border. Whatever the location, these gardens should achieve a wild, untamed look. Plants can be combined with domestic perennials. With these gardens, there is virtually no maintenance, except for an occasional feeding and removal of dead stalks before new growth appears in the spring. Plant growth should remain free, unless plants become unhealthy because of overcrowding or disease.

Another aspect of wildgarden planting is creating new prairie lands by using a wide spectrum of native flowers and grasses. Seed producers are now selling a wide range of wild plant seed mixtures. Many of these mixtures are good for erosion control in addition to being a natural cover for wildlife.

Because of the large number of wildflowers now offered, it is impossible to show them all. However, those we have chosen are dependable, attractive and most

BLOODROOT

SNOW TRILLIUM

BUTTERFLY VIOLET

like a woodland setting.

The tallest of this group at 2' (60cm) is Marsh Marigold, *Caltha palustris,* which produces golden yellow flowers in early spring. This is a good plant for stream banks because of the need for a continually moist, acidic soil. Marsh Marigold does best in full sun, but tolerates open shade.

Erythronium americanum, or Fawnlily, is a yellow flowering woodland plant, producing its daylily like blooms in spring. This plant prefers moist, acidic soil, and a partially shaded location. Height ranges from 4-10" (10-25cm).

Bloodroot, *Sanguinea canadensis,* is another low grower, producing white delicate ray style flowers. This rhizomatous perennial flowers in spring. It is a woodland plant that prefers a moist, organic soil of acidic pH. Height remains under 12" (30cm).

Snow Trillium, or *Trillium grandiflorum* is a three petaled wildflower that bears snowy white flowers for several weeks in spring. Flowers change from white to pink, then rose as they wither. It is a clump forming plant, sending up 6-8 stems at a time, which range from 8-16" (20-40cm). Red fruits are produced in autumn and foliage is a clear green. Trilliums do well in light to deep shade, where

soil is continuously moist and rich in organic matter.

Among those that can form a lush woodland carpet is Butterfly Violet, *Viola papilionacea,* although it performs best in open shade. Flowers range from purple to white and large basally produced heart-shaped leaves create a clump-shaped plant sometimes nearly 12" (30cm) tall and wide. It does best in moist sandy soil.

Hardy ferns, though not wildflowers, are native plants that can provide foil for blooming natives. Most need moist soil although some tolerate dry conditions, if there is shade.

Interrupted Fern, *Osmunda claytonia,* is a robust kind that does well in either moist or dry shaded soils. Woolly foliage of early spring becomes smooth later in the season. Height and spread ranges from 2-4' (60-120cm).

Another large hardy variety is Lady Fern, *Athyrium filix femina.* This is one of the most easy to grow and very attractive. Like other ferns, it needs a moist soil high in organic matter, but can take more sun than most.

Remember that local growers and garden centers handle wildflowers and other native plants that perform well in their areas. Their recommendations will save disappointment.

PERENNIALS, BULBS, CONIFERS AND BROADLEAF EVERGREENS USED IN A ROCK GARDEN SITUATION.

HOW TO USE HARDY BULBS WITH PERENNIALS

Because many hardy bulbs are the first flowers of spring, their most important function in the perennial garden is to extend the season. Most perennials are in various growth stages during early spring months, but have not yet produced blooms.

Earliest flowering of hardy bulbs are dwarf novelty items including Snowdrops, *Galanthus nivalis;* Crocus, various species; Hyacinth, *Hyacinthus orientalis;* Grape Hyacinth, *Muscari armeniacum;* Siberian Squill, *Scilla sibirica;* Greek Anemone, *Anemone blanda;* Glory of the Snow, *Chionodoxa luciliae;* Winter aconite, *Eranthis hyemalis;* and species Tulips.

Snowdrops appear in late winter, producing small white flowers on 4" (10cm) stems. They like sunny, moist soils protected from wind. Somewhat taller is Glory of the Snow producing brilliant blue flowers with white centers.

Also only a few inches tall is Siberian Squill, producing vivid blue flowers and rush like leaves. These are good for planting beneath shrubs. Bulbs increase rapidly, creating a showy colony after a few seasons. Another prolific dwarf is Grape Hyacinth producing grapelike clusters of tiny round blue or white bells.

The spring flowering crocus encompasses 11 major families. Goblet-shaped flowers are produced on short stems in early spring and come in a wide color range. Large golden stamens enhance their beauty.

Crocus like a sunny location that is protected from wind. Also liking a sunny, wind protected location is Winter Aconite, which after several years, will carpet a wide area with small golden yellow flowers. Flowers are produced on 2-4" (5-10cm) stems and rich green or bronze foliage is finely divided.

MUSCARI, FOREGROUND, WITH NARCISSUS

ANEMONE BLUE STAR

GLORY OF THE SNOW

TURKESTAN TULIP

CROCUS

SNOWDROPS

At 9" (23cm), Hyacinths produce large cone-shaped flower heads in a blue, pink, white, yellow and lavender. Rich green foliage is produced from the plant's base. It also likes a protected location and well-drained soil.

Early flowering species tulips include members of *Tulipa fosteriana, T. kaufmanniana, T. clusiana* and *T. turkestanica.* Of the four, *T. fosteriana* is the tallest growing 14-20" (35-50cm). *T. kaufmanniana* is known as the Waterlily Tulip, producing large flowers on short stems. When blooms are open, they resemble waterlilies. *T. clusiana* is commonly known as Lady Tulip. It grows 12" (30cm) tall. Blooms are striped pink and white. Also of unusual coloration is *Tulipa turkestanica,* producing ivory blooms with dark centers.

In the perennial garden, dwarf hardy bulbs work well as edging although later flowering low-growing perennials should be planted nearby to hide withering foliage following the bloom period. If possible, this practice should also be done in the rock garden.

In natural settings, spring bulbs appear to be native plants. Most widely used are the somewhat later flowering daffodils, which put on a brilliant show along a forest border, near a fence or in a meadow setting. The tech-nique for making bulbs appear natural is to scatter a number in a given area and plant them where they fall.

In groundcovers, hardy bulbs also make a nice early spring show. Brilliant blooms appear through a mantle of green. The groundcover then blooms later in spring, providing continuing interest. The green groundcover also hides dying foliage of early flowering bulbs. This technique usually works best for daffodils and early flowering tulips, because dwarf bulbs will not be tall enough to be seen.

Tall growing tulips, narcissus, and *Scilla hispanica* are usually recommended for showy mass plantings, either in a bulb garden or as part of the perennial garden.

All spring flowering bulbs should be planted in the fall, where there is moist, but well-drained soil. Keep in mind that these bulbs do not need fertilizing, but can use some bone meal at planting time. Fertilize after foliage appears in the spring.

Regardless of planting site, it is wise to consider exposure to sunlight, because most bulbs do better in full sun. However, because so many bloom before leaves on shrubs and trees appear in spring, locations shaded later in the growing season are usually suitable.

CROSS REFERENCE INDEX

PLANT HARDINESS ZONES

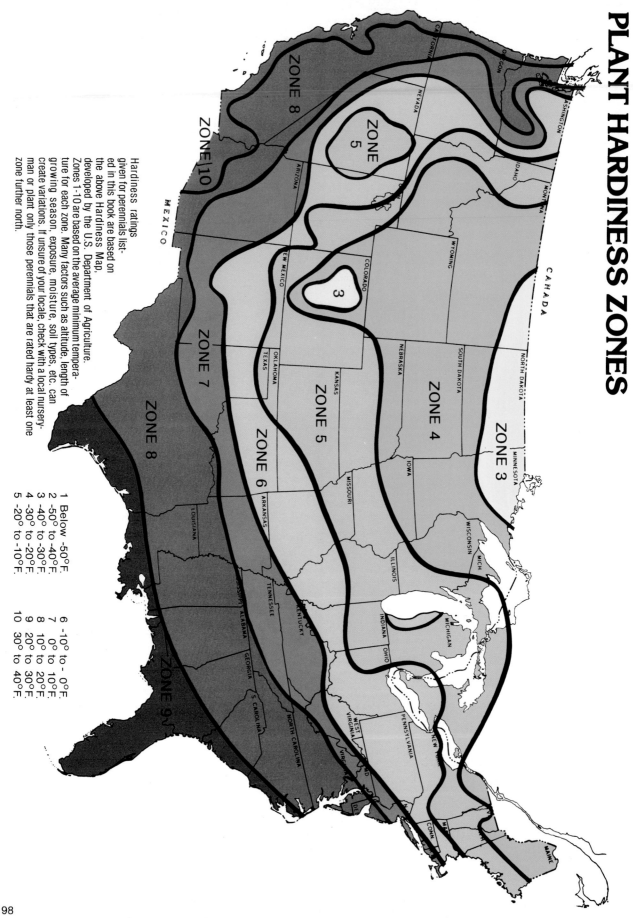

Hardiness ratings
given for perennials listed in this book are based on
the above Hardiness Map,
developed by the U.S. Department of Agriculture.
Zones 1-10 are based on the average minimum tempera-
ture for each zone. Many factors such as altitude, length of
growing season, exposure, moisture, soil types, etc. can
create variations. If unsure of your locale, check with a local nurseryman or plant only those perennials that are rated hardy at least one
zone further north.

1 Below -50°F.
2 -50° to -40°F.
3 -40° to -30°F.
4 -30° to -20°F.
5 -20° to -10°F.

6 -10° to - 0°F.
7 0° to 10°F.
8 10° to 20°F.
9 20° to 30°F.
10 30° to 40°F.

ZONE 8
ZONE 10
ZONE 5
ZONE 3
ZONE 7
ZONE 8
ZONE 6
ZONE 5
ZONE 4
ZONE 3
ZONE 9